Adrenal F
Don't Let It Keep Y
Weight and Enjoy...

INSTITUTE

Written By
The Adrenal Fatigue Institute

A Tri-Star Publishing Book

Adrenal Fatigue
Don't Let It Keep You from Losing Weight and Enjoying Life

Published by:
Tri-Star Publications Inc
P.O. Box 18653
West Palm Beach, FL 33416-8653

First Tri-Star Publishing Printing, December 2007

ISBN: 0-9802188-0-2

INSTITUTE
Trademark Adrenal fatigue Institute

Printed in the United States of America

Publishers Note- Disclaimer:

Adrenal Fatigue

Don't Let It Keep You from Losing Weight and Enjoying Life

Table of Contents:

Does this Sound Familiar?

**Many sources of stress come at all hours of the day.
The body has little time to relax and repair.**

Stress. At one point in each of our lives, there comes a period where all of the little things start to pile up. If you are like most Americans, you probably remember your youth as carefree times, when you had little responsibility, and the biggest concern you had was the date planned for Saturday night. As these days faded into distant memory, many Americans find themselves caught in a seemingly endless race.

Our mornings are usually a marathon of routines and rituals: hitting the 'snooze' button a few times for an extra twenty minutes of sleep, rushing through errands hoping to get out of the house a few minutes early, maybe grabbing a quick cup of coffee and a breakfast sandwich at the local fast-food restaurant. Only on rare days do you make it out early enough to beat the traffic, congestion, accidents, and seemingly growing rate of road rage. Once you make it to work, you throw yourself through a gauntlet of endless tasks and projects, required to meet stringent deadlines to preserve some sense of job security. You then take a quick lunch break, typically the minimum amount of time that state labor laws require, just enough to down a sandwich and a soda or two. By the end of the day, you are exhausted, left to face the same nightmare on the roads that stressed you that morning. You then might retreat to your home, reassuring yourself that tonight will be different; tonight you will take the time to relax and enjoy your down time. But, you come home only to see the bills piling up on the counter; you've got to address the problem that your child had at school; your spouse is equally stressed and ready to snap. By the time you've taken care of everything, there might be a chance to catch a few minutes of late-night television as you unwind and try to force yourself to sleep at a decent hour.

One of the most significant problems that most Americans face each day is the battery of stress that almost attacks us from every angle. While you may think that you are strong and personally able to face constant stressors without any problems, your body might not agree. You might be mentally able to handle constant stressors, but these stressors still trigger your body to function in stress mode. While science and private industry has turned out an almost infinite number of inventions, tools, electronics, and even drugs, each designed to improve our lifestyle, all they seem to do is make life more-fast paced.

The problem with today's lifestyle is that there are millions of products and businesses that provide convenience. But with each convenience comes a significant cost. Fast-food tastes great and is cheap and available in mere minutes, but the nutrients are severely lacking and it's loaded with saturated fats, sugars, and excessive calories. Computers continue to become faster and smarter than most of us need, but rather than allowing us to work more leisurely, we are now expected to perform more work in the same amount of time.

While our tools, equipment, and foods have become faster and smarter, the basic chemistry of the human body has remained the same. We can always work longer, work harder, even work smarter, but the human body was not designed to handle this to the degree to which society often demands.

With a barrage of stress, lack of exercise, unbalanced diet, and a day-to-day lifestyle that leaves little time to relax, your body is may be ready to call it quits! Most of us get a week or two of vacation time per year, hoping that this little time will be enough to unwind and recharge. If this is you, then your body may be in trouble.

One of the most overlooked and often, overworked systems of the human body are the Adrenal System. This may sound familiar because you probably have heard of adrenaline, which is exclusively controlled by the Adrenal Glands, but how much do you really know about your Adrenal System?

While adrenaline is mostly utilized as the primary energy source during an emergency (i.e. that rush of excitement, fast heart rate, and surge of energy you get before a close call that almost resulted in a traffic accident, or when a housewife is able to lift the front end of a car as it pins her child to the ground), the Adrenal Glands are also solely responsible for the production and management of cortisol, which is the body's primary defense system to help fight stress. In addition, the

Adrenal Glands greatly influence the body's ability to maintain steady energy throughout the day.

Most of us overstress the Adrenal Glands everyday through poor diet, intake of caffeine and other stimulants, stress, lack of sleep, and other energy robbing activities. But when was the last time that you took a minute to refresh this over-taxed system?

Generally speaking, as the Adrenal System continues to be over-taxed, it eventually is unable to keep up with production. Like a production line that is severely under-staffed, the Adrenal Glands can only function for so long above their means until production suffers. When the Adrenal System is unable to function completely, it is unable to manage the energy that your lifestyle is demanding. As the Adrenal Glands fatigue, their production of response hormones decline and there are generally a few tell-tale signs signaling trouble is on the horizon.

Do any of these sound familiar to you?
- Morning fatigue. Not seeming to "wake up" until 10 am even though you've been up for 3 hours.
- Middle of the afternoon "Low". Sluggishness and clouded thinking in the middle of the day.
- Burst of energy around 6 pm
- Sleepiness around 9pm, but a "Second Energy Burst" from around 11 pm to 1 am. You may find it difficult to fall asleep between these times.
- Mild depression, decreased sex drive, lack of energy and lack of focus/concentration
- Muscular weakness and declining endurance

- Weight gain (especially around the midsection), with extreme difficulty in losing it
- Unrelaxing or unfulfilling sleep

While I'm sure most of us can relate to a few of these, it's scary to think that many people suffer from 3 or more of these warning signs. Even worse is that some of you can relate to ALL of these!

The most significant causes of Adrenal Fatigue are constant physical and/or emotional stress, the over-use of stimulants and nicotine, lack of exercise, and a poor diet. For most people, Adrenal Fatigue is caused by a combination of each of these factors; however, everyone responds to each of these stressors differently. It is even possible to reach this stage with minimal or zero caffeine and stimulant intake; with the right combination of physical/emotional stressors, lack of sleep, and poor lifestyle, it's just as easy to burn out your Adrenal Glands while stimulant-free. Some people feel little effects from physical or emotional stress, yet their lack of exercise, stimulant abuse, and poor diet are the key contributors in damaging their Adrenal Glands. It is important to realize that you might think that you handle stress well, but truly, it takes a major toll on the body. There are not always clear-cut signs that the body is facing stress.

Have you ever caught yourself at work, going at a fast pace for quite a while, when you suddenly realize that you have been sitting uncomfortably for some time? This is something that many of us do every day, and it's a tell-tale sign that we are forcing our body into a stressful situation to try to accomplish a task in a given time.

As the Adrenal Glands fatigue, you may also notice some signs of depression as your energy decreases. You might have trouble staying motivated, your outlook on life is somewhat grim, you become irritable over minor things, you have difficulty thinking or concentrating, and you have a disinterest in many hobbies or pleasurable activities, including sex. Besides symptoms of depression, you are probably noticing increased weight gain, and are finding it hard to shed this fat.

Why is all of this happening? Is this just normal signs of aging? The answer is no.

In the next few chapters we will cover how your Adrenal System serves almost like the body's 'Command Center', how small changes can greatly improve your energy levels, and simple diet and lifestyle changes that can help you feel young and vibrant.

What is the Adrenal System?

Adrenal Fatigue is a somewhat complex issue, yet explained in steps, it can be easy to understand. Many people outside of the health industry get somewhat overwhelmed at over-scientific approaches, so we will illustrate the Adrenal System and all of the components of Adrenal Fatigue from their basics. This will allow you to have a full understanding of the components at work, the mechanisms of action, and how this can be treated.

Where are your Adrenal Glands? When asked this, many people point to their neck (possibly confusing Adrenal Glands with their Thyroid), but the Adrenal Glands are located in your abdomen above the kidneys.

The Adrenal System

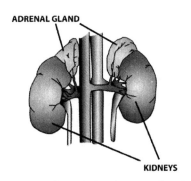

ADRENAL GLAND

KIDNEYS

Your body has 2 Adrenal Glands: One triangle-shaped gland sits atop each kidney. Both play a major role in energy production and hormone regulation.

These glands are part of the endocrine system, which is a system of glands throughout your body responsible for the release of hormones.

As a whole, the endocrine system is responsible for regulating metabolism, energy production, and even significant in controlling many aspects of your mood.

Nearly everyone has heard of hormones before, most are familiar with testosterone and estrogen, as these are the hormones that differentiate men from women, but what is a hormone? A hormone is a chemical messenger that signals the body's cells. There are many hormones in the body, but hormones are responsible for almost everything that happens in the body such as immune function, metabolism, growth, mood, energy, sex, reproduction, and more.

Each of the Adrenal Glands are made up of two key parts, the first part, the Adrenal medulla, is the center, or core of the gland. The Adrenal medulla is responsible for the creation and release of adrenaline and noradrenaline. It is also the body's main source of dopamine. A normal functioning Adrenal System is important as the release of dopamine in the brain has been shown to play an important role in cognition, motor function, motivation, sleep, mood, attention, and learning. If your adrenal function is repressed and your dopamine levels are lower than normal, you may experience symptoms of depression, fatigue, and lack of motivation. Proper dopamine levels are one of the key components in maintaining a positive outlook on life.

The adrenal medulla makes other hormones including epinephrine and norepinephrine. These hormones control the body's responses to stress, including the "fight-or-flight" adrenaline surge when you face danger or stress.

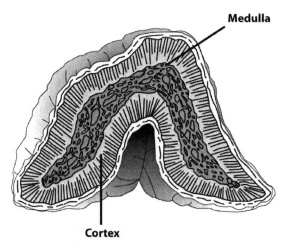

Medulla

Cortex

**Illustrated is the two parts of the Adrenal Gland:
the Adrenal Cortex and the Adrenal Medulla, both key
producers of vital hormones as well as energy production.**

The outer part of the Adrenal Gland is the Adrenal cortex, which produces a number of different hormones such as cortisol, aldosterone, and dehydroepiandrosterone (DHEA). These hormones carefully control metabolism and other characteristics such as hair growth, and body shape.

DHEA is often called the mother hormone since it has the ability to convert into sex hormones such as testosterone and estrogen as needed. Studies have shown that DHEA is increased with regular exercise, but the average adult produces about 25mgs a day. Adequate levels of DHEA are needed to ensure your body can produce the proper amount of hormones it needs to function properly. When the body's hormones are balanced, your mood is constant and you feel lucid, pleasant and enthusiastic. DHEA is considered by many to be the best "feel-good" hormone in the body. When DHEA levels are low due to improper adrenal function, your body cannot regulate proper bodily function. Improper hormone production can cause you to experience a sense of depression and melancholy.

One of the main hormones produced by the Adrenal System is Cortisol. While Cortisol is an essential hormone, if its levels are not balanced in the body, it can cause serious health concerns. Cortisol is the primary stress hormone. Its primary function is to restore homeostasis (stability) after stress. To accomplish this task, Cortisol raises blood pressure, increases blood sugar, weakens the immune system, slows the metabolism, and even impairs memory and thinking. While these are all negative effects, in an emergency these drastic changes help the body to eliminate, escape, or cope with stress. Cortisol is essential for survival, but chronically elevated Cortisol levels can severely hinder your health.

When you are stressed, your body releases Cortisol to help control the stress response, but what happens when you are constantly stressed? Cortisol levels remain elevated.

Looking at Cortisol's functions, you can see why elevated levels of this hormone are very bad for your health. Not only will it cause you to gain weight, it hinders your metabolism, and can even weaken your immune system. This formula makes you susceptible to illness while also making it next to impossible to control your weight.

While Cortisol can damage the body, it is necessary in its intended dose. Cortisol is essential for controlling blood sugar levels through its ability to control Insulin. Serving as the primary hormone in response to stress, our bodies need Cortisol to survive emergencies. In the past, some products have attempted to cure stress-induced weight gain by blocking or eliminating Cortisol. Without Cortisol, your Insulin levels would remain elevated for hours after eating, and Insulin signals the body to pack food (glucose) into the cells. This will again, just lead to weight gain. Rather than eliminate Cortisol, the healthy way to control weight, energy, sleep, and mood is to allow Cortisol to function in the body within the normal realm of its function. We want Cortisol, just not too much or too little.

Factors that Affect the Adrenal Glands

There are several lifestyle factors that can significantly influence or modify Adrenal function. When you increase the normal functioning of the Adrenal Glands, you force the glands to increase output, produce more energy, and increase the output of stress and response hormones. With minor stress reactions, this is a normal process as it is what the Adrenal Glands were designed to do. When you give your body adequate time to recover, the Adrenal Glands are able to resort back to normal functioning as well as normal energy production. When the Adrenal Glands are not given the time and tools necessary to recover, they may weaken over time and their functionality may become exhausted. Sleep is essential for recovery, repair, and maintenance of the body. Without proper sleep quality and quantity, the body never gets the 'vacation' that it needs.

Your Adrenal System is greatly influenced by the foods and drinks you consume. By definition, all stimulants such as caffeine and nicotine are drugs. These stimulants have the ability to increase the activity of the central nervous system and/or the sympathetic nervous system.

For instance, let's look at a stimulant that everyone is familiar with: caffeine. Caffeine is a natural substance as it is found in over 60 plants. Interesting enough, plants naturally produce caffeine for protection purposes; it works as a natural pesticide since it has the potency to either kill or paralyze certain insects as they attempt to feed on the plant.

The caffeine that you and I most commonly consume is extracted from the beans of the coffee plant and/or the leaves of tea bushes. When you consume caffeine, it is absorbed within the stomach and small intestine. It generally takes 15 minutes for caffeine to produce its stimulating effects.

Just how long does that cup of coffee stay in your system?
Science commonly refers to the term 'half-life' when referring to the length of time that it takes for the body to eliminate something from the body. Half-life refers to the amount of time that it takes to eliminate 50% of the initial dose. If the half life is 3 hours, this does not mean that 100% will be eliminated in 6 hours.

Since the half-life of caffeine is about 3 hours, it will take 3 hours for 50% of the caffeine in your system to be eliminated. If you consume 100mg of caffeine at noon, at 3pm there is still 50mg of caffeine in your body. Over the next 3 hours (3pm to 6pm), 50% of the current 50mg will be eliminated leaving 25mg active caffeine at 6pm. At 9pm, there will still be about 12.5mg of caffeine in your body,

The half-life of caffeine depends greatly on many factors including your age, medication, pregnancy, and your liver function (the liver is responsible for metabolizing caffeine).

On average, the half-life of caffeine is 3-4 hours in a healthy adult. However, this number almost doubles (5-10 hours) in women taking oral contraceptives. What this means is that every 3-4 hours, 50% of the caffeine in your system is being eliminated. As you can see in the illustrated chart, after consuming a 100mg dose of caffeine (the average cup of coffee), it can take upwards of 15 hours before the caffeine is entirely metabolized. The higher dose you consume, the longer that the process will take.

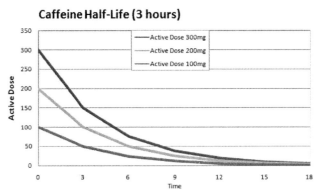

So, when you have a soda or cup of coffee in the afternoon, there are stimulants still in your system when you go to bed that evening. You can see how stimulants earlier in the day have the ability to contribute to sleep disorders.

There's no question that caffeine and other stimulants have some very attractive benefits to us. They allow us to work faster, be more alert, typically raise our mood, alleviate headaches, and reduce our awareness of stress. But with most benefits, comes compromise.

Stimulants such as caffeine can play a significant role in your body's Adenosine management. Adenosine plays a vital role in energy transfer, as well as essential role in biochemical processes, such as signal transduction as cyclic adenosine monophosphate (cAMP). In other words, **Adenosine is your body's energy control center.** Adenosine is also an inhibitory neurotransmitter, which plays a major role in promoting deep refreshing sleep and suppressing the body's tendency to get restless sleep. When adenosine is not received properly in the body, energy levels decrease and sleep quality can decrease.

The effects of adenosine have been shown to be significantly blunted in individuals who are taking large quantities of stimulants like caffeine, green tea, Nicotine and Amphetamines.

Adenosine works in the body though a series of receptors that are called A1 and A2 Receptors. These receptors are essential to your health because they regulate Adenosine levels. As illustrated below, prolonged exposure to stimulants can cause significant concerns for several reasons. In structure, the caffeine molecule is similar to adenosine, allowing caffeine to cause up-regulation or buffering of the receptor. The buffering that occurs on your A1 and A2 receptors from abusing stimulants like caffeine, ephedra, amphetamines and nicotine causes Adenosine to be blocked, severely limiting your ability to function from 'natural' energy.

Upregulation of A1 (Energy) Receptors From Stimulant Abuse

a. **No Damage:** Caffeine and natural energy production are equally recieved.
b. **Moderate Damage:** Stimulant abuse begins blocking natural energy production.
c. **Extensive Damage:** Natural energy (adenosine) is mostly ineffective, more stimulants are needed in order to feel energized.

For example caffeine's stimulatory effects are primarily (although not completely) credited to its inhibition of adenosine by attaching to the same receptors (A1 and A2). By nature of caffeine's chemical structure, it's attaching effectively blocks adenosine receptors in the central nervous system. This reduction in adenosine activity through the buffering of these receptors leads to the fatigue, lack of energy, and the depression one experiences from Adrenal fatigue.

Stimulants can greatly contribute to Adrenal Fatigue. But is it possible to suffer from Adrenal Fatigue symptoms without even consuming stimulants? You better believe it. We'll get to that next.

Lifestyle Contributions

Stimulants are not the only things that have an effect on adrenal health. While stimulants can be the easiest target, an equal, if not greater amount of damage can be contributed by your lifestyle.

As we covered, the Adrenal Glands are responsible for the 'fight-or-flight' response that is one of the most important tools in human survival. The 'fight-or-flight' response is the triggered reaction that you face when you stand in certain danger. Chemical reactions take place within milliseconds and the body quickly reacts to the danger at hand.

When the body is stressed, and the 'fight –or-flight' response is triggered, the body responds quickly:
- Heart rate increases
- Veins and arteries allow maximum blood-flow
- Breathing rate accelerates to bring oxygen to the lungs and muscles faster
- Fat and sugars are metabolized to create instant energy
- Pupils dilate to allow better vision
- The digestive system is slowed to conserve energy
- Sweat glands are activated
- Endorphins are released
- Mental judgment / clarity is delayed

This is interesting because the body reacts to daily stressors in a similar way. When the body is mentally or emotionally stressed, it releases hormones to try to combat the situation and maintain homeostasis, or a stable, constant condition (i.e. normal functioning). Look at it this way: the body is like two equal-weighted children sitting on a see-saw.

When neither child pushes against the ground, the see-saw is perfectly balanced, each side remains the same distance from the ground, and the see-saw does not move. But when one child pushes against the ground, his side goes up, forcing the other child to drop to the ground. As the other child responds, pushing his side sky-high, he is lowered to the ground again by the first child.

The body in a state of homeostasis:
The body is in harmony as the Adrenal Glands
function normally.

When in harmony, the body is like the still and balanced see-saw. All bodily functions continue to operate in their normal modes, and neither side moves. Imagine stress as a heavy weight on one side. As the stress grows, the body (the other side of the see-saw) raises higher into the sky. The body immediately reacts to this to bring itself back into harmony: stress hormones are released (i.e. Cortisol), certain bodily functions such as breathing and/or heart rate are altered to meet the demand, and the body fights to respond to the factor that is displacing harmony. As the body reacts, it overcompensates, shooting its side to the ground. However, this is a short lived gain, within no time, the stress side fights back, forcing the body's side back to the sky.

The body in a state of continual stress:
As constant stressors affect the body, the Adrenal Glands are
forced to work overtime and often cannot keep up with demand.

This process will continue until one of two things happens: the body exhausts or the stress is relieved. While this cycle is a little dramatic, imagine all of the minor stressors in your day piling on the side against your harmony. As the day starts with the morning traffic, the red light you seem to get stuck at everyday, your workload at the office, etc; you do get a few minutes for lunch, but is it really enough to counter the assault of stressors?

Not for most of us. The day continues, the stressors continue to pile up. Finally you retreat to your home, only to be barraged by another assault of stressors. While the work stressors are typically mechanical, (i.e. they are things that can be solved with time and some thought) the home stressors are typically entirely emotional, (i.e. they revolve around money, your family, and things that you don't have complete or any control over. Any parent with a teenager in the house can attribute to this).

Now, stress alone will place a significant toll on your Adrenal System, but on its own, it may or may not necessarily be enough to completely damage Adrenal function. But, stress is just another piece of the pie that causes Adrenal Fatigue.

When was your last good night's sleep? And no, I do not mean the last time that you got 8 hours of uninterrupted sleep. It's easy to have 8+ hours of sleep, yet still wake up groggy or un-refreshed. When was the last time you woke up, jumped out of bed, and felt completely refreshed; a morning when you didn't need anything to get going? You were ready to face the day without the help of a cold shower or cup of coffee.

Sleep is one of the most important aspects of our lives, yet we seem to give it the least amount of attention. Most of us sleep on 12 year old mattresses, flat pillows, and get far too little sleep per night. The notion of 'catching up' on the weekends is almost as farfetched as putting this book under your pillow at night and expecting to have it committed to memory by morning.

Sleep is the only true resting period that your body gets. It is the body's only time to repair, grow, and relax. Think about how much brain activity it takes just to read this sentence. Muscles in your eyes scan the paper as your pupils adjust to the light in the room and the retina transmits the characters to a series of nerves that transmit the findings to the brain. Your brain recognizes the characters, translates their meaning, and creates ideas and emotions based upon the text. Simultaneously, your hands are holding the book steady, other muscles are holding your posture up so you can sit without keeling over, your breathing is steady, and your blood is pumping through miles of veins, arteries and capillaries. At the same time, your brain is aware of the temperature of the room, the texture of your clothes, the comfort of the chair, or background noises. Your brain is constantly working all day long. Even when you are doing the most mundane tasks, there are millions of processes going on each second.

Once you consider the abuse that your brain goes through all day long just for you to be able to function smoothly, don't you think that relaxing sleep might be the least that you can do for it?

Consider the intensified impact that stimulants and stress place on your body each day. The human body was engineered to reset during the hours of sleep. Some people need 8 hours of sleep per night; others operate great after only 6. We do accept that everyone is similar at their core, yet we must identify the fact that every person is completely different. While the duration of hours that you sleep uninterrupted is extremely important, the most important factor in restful sleep is the quality of the sleep.

Think of your Adrenal Glands as your cell-phone's battery. When your phone is on, yet it is not in use, many phones will have enough reserve to last 3 or 4 days straight. But what happens when you spend just a few hours on the phone? Suddenly, the battery indicator drops, and you are forced to charge it in the middle of the day, or every night at the least.

When was your last actual vacation. I'm not talking about the trip to your in-laws last winter. Remember that relaxing week at the lake, or the resort at the beach. Most likely, this was the last stress-free day that you had. Work, bills, errands -- they were all put off and your mind was at ease. Unless you are one of the privileged few who can financially afford to live in a perpetual state of vacation, a stress-free vacation is a luxury that comes all too seldom. But with gas prices climbing to record highs, hours lost in security checks and delays at airports, work that follows you outside the office, even a vacation can be a nightmare.

As days and weeks seem to run into one another, how much time do you take each day to take a deep breath, close your eyes, and escape the grasp of stress for a few minutes? For many of us, the only down-time in the day is the few hours set aside for sleep. As America's job market becomes more and more competitive with each wave of graduating college students becoming more tech savvy, many of us are forced to work ten times harder and longer just to keep up. Down time means a lack of productivity and most bosses don't look highly upon cat-naps at your desk. The ironic part is that a 15-minute cat nap in the afternoon would greatly increase most people's productivity for the latter part of the day and could easily make up for the missed time.

So, as you continue to live and constantly push yourself at a greater pace just to keep up, your body continues to work harder and harder, trying to provide the energy and mental ingenuity for you to succeed. Most of us take for granted the endurance that our Adrenal Glands provide for us daily. Yet, after a barrage of stimulants from coffee, sodas, and diet pills; running a gauntlet of tasks and projects at work without taking adequate time to relax; and a home life that is typically far from relaxing, at this point your Adrenal Glands may be exhausted.

Adrenal Fatigue: What's Really Going On

After covering the basics of the Adrenal System, and how your lifestyle contributes to Adrenal health, let's explore what happens when your Adrenal System is unable to perform at its prime. Adrenal Fatigue is not something that manifests itself overnight. As the Adrenal System is stressed and forced into overproduction for an extended period of time, the Adrenal System goes through a cycle as it attempts to compensate with the stressors. Unable to output beyond its means, the Adrenal Gland eventually 'gives up' and its production of essential hormones is severely limited.

This process can vary in length due to the varied number and severity of stressors that each of us is under. While the length of time may vary, the characteristics of Adrenal Fatigue are similar. There are 3 basic phases of Adrenal Fatigue.

Phase 1: Initial Exposure

The initial phase of Adrenal Fatigue is the Initial Expose to the stressor or group of stressors that place the extra toll on your Adrenal System. For many, this phase is introduced by a major life occurrence or a new stage in life: death of a loved one, a high stress job, marriage, childbirth, school, etc. While the exact source of this will vary for each person, this can be any event that greatly alters one's lifestyle or day-to-day activities.

For example, childbirth is one of the most joyous occasions in our lives, but consider the life altering factors that are involved:
Fear of being a new parent, fear of disability or disease, stress of bills and debt, fearful of losing free-time and sense of one's self, enormous

joy and excitement, substantial lifestyle alterations, change of sleep schedule, etc.

In most cases, the excitement and joy will greatly overcome the fears that we have, but in either case, the brain is still reacting to each of these greatly varied emotions. Whenever you feel an emotion, whether it be fear, joy, anger, depression, guilt, or love, your body copes with this emotion through signaling hormones. Each emotion is accompanied by some change in body functioning such as a change in blood pressure, heart beat, or 'chill through the spine'.

In normal amounts, the body reacts to stress and overcomes it once the stressor is eliminated or you become accustomed to the situation. With major lifestyle changes, we often find ourselves in a situation in which we are unable to comfortably adjust to the new scenario. This is the case with new parent when they sacrifice a few hours of sleep per night, a new promotion has an employee working longer and harder to prove his value, or a widow is suddenly left with a void in her life. Since we are unable to swiftly overcome these stressors, they often begin to follow us day-in and day-out, with little relief.

What Happens to Your Body in Phase 1?

During the Initial Exposure stage of Adrenal Fatigue, the Adrenal System begins producing higher levels of Cortisol in response to the elevated stress levels.

As mentioned before, Cortisol has the ability to raise blood pressure, increase blood sugar, weaken the immune system, slow the metabolism, and even impair memory and thinking. In response to normal, short-lived stress, Cortisol is essential for re-establishing stability after stress; however, consistently elevated Cortisol levels in response to perpetual stress can have devastating effects on the body.

The thyroid is one of the essential components of your metabolism and the processes that control the calories that you burn, and essentially how much of your food is converted into fat. High levels of Cortisol will lower Thyroid-Stimulating-Hormone (TSH) and reduce the output of the Thyroid. This will ultimately cause weight gain, even though you eat the same foods and live the same lifestyle.

Cortisol is also the key player in regulating Insulin levels. Insulin is the hormone that is primarily responsible for turning the food you eat into energy for your cells. Most organisms on the planet use Insulin and it is impossible for man to live without it. Shortly after you consume a meal, the food is converted into sugar (glucose) and Insulin is released to signal the cells to absorb the sugar. In order to 'turn-off' the effects of Insulin, the body secretes Cortisol, which is an antagonist of Insulin and has the ability to stop its effects in the body.

Elevated Cortisol levels can also cause Hyperglycemia. While Insulin signals the cells to absorb glucose, Cortisol does the opposite. Typically used for a source of energy during an emergency, Cortisol elevates blood-glucose levels. When blood-glucose (blood-sugar) levels remain elevated for too long, the body enters the state of Hyperglycemia.

High Cortisol levels also require more Insulin to perform the same task. Quite often, this results in Insulin Resistance, in which the body becomes somewhat 'immune' to normal Insulin levels, requiring a larger dose to achieve the same goal.

While the hormones that control your glucose levels lose balance, other Adrenal functions are simultaneously limited. Along with this imbalance comes a diminished production of DHEA. As mentioned previously, DHEA is often called the mother hormone for its ability to convert into testosterone and estrogens as needed. Adequate levels of DHEA are needed to ensure your body can produce the amount of hormones it needs to function properly. When the body's hormones are balanced, your mood is constant and you feel lucid, pleasant and enthusiastic. DHEA is considered by many to be the best "feel-good" hormone in the body. When DHEA levels are low due to improper adrenal function, your body cannot regulate ideal endocrine proper bodily function. Improper hormone production can cause you to experience a sense of depression and melancholy.

Phase 2: Adrenal Fatigue

Cortisol levels can only remain elevated for so long before the Adrenal Glands are unable to retain elevated Cortisol production. This stage is characterized by the decline of Cortisol levels. Once the Adrenal Glands are completely unable to continue their output of Cortisol, the body is without an energy source to handle stress or control Insulin levels.

As DHEA levels continue to decline, the body's testosterone and estrogen levels continue to decrease. Since testosterone and estrogen are both essential in both men and women (but in different ratios), a drop in either of these can have dramatic effects for anyone.

Since Estrogen and Testosterone are both vital in both sexes for controlling sex drive and functioning, most people (both men and women) will have very little sexual appetite and/or inability to perform during this phase. In addition to sexual health, low DHEA levels are also associated with lower bone density, diminished immune system, depression, and other dehabilitating effects.

To reverse this scenario, it can take more than just relieving the stressor. Since the body has undergone significant changes in functioning, it is important that the individual take diet, exercise, and a healthy lifestyle into consideration at this stage. If the body is fueled with over-processed foods and other choices that exclude a wide array of vitamins, minerals, and antioxidants, the Adrenal System will be unable to return to normal functioning. A full recovery from this stage will vary in length, but it can take several months to restore proper function.

Phase 3: Adrenal Shutdown
If the cycle of Adrenal Fatigue continues, and the individual fails to relieve him or herself from the source of chronic stress, the Adrenal System will continue in a downward spiral until it reaches shutdown. At this stage, the Adrenal System will not be entirely turned off, but it has been greatly reduced in comparison to its ideal operation. Typically, it will take years of stress, stimulant abuse, lack of sleep, and poor diet in order to fully reach this state of Adrenal Fatigue. The most important issue to consider when recovering from this Phase is that it is not possible to fully repair the Adrenal System in a short period of time. Just as it took months or years to reach this level of Adrenal Fatigue, it is impractical to think that this can be repaired in a matter of days or weeks.

As a result of hormonal deficiency, persons who are in this Phase of Adrenal Fatigue will have drastically low levels of energy, lack of patience, limited physical and mental endurance, low motivation, poor mood, severe sugar and salt cravings, almost nonexistent libido, and significant weight gain.

The most important step in approaching Adrenal recovery from this Phase of Adrenal Fatigue is eliminating negativities in your life. Whether your stress may stem from work, financial issues, marital troubles, or another significant stressor, you must confront these issues and explore other options to reduce their impact on your health. This does not mean that you have to quit your job, leave your spouse, or rob a bank, but rather to identify what you can do in each scenario to highlight the positive elements and reduce the negativities.

Although exercise is vital for your health, strenuous exercise can cause further damage to persons in this Phase of Adrenal Fatigue. Strenuous exercises such as heavy weight lifting, long periods of cardio, or other activities should be limited. Non-strenuous exercises such as lifting light to moderate weights, light cardio (mild to moderate intensity lasting less than 30-45 minutes), or playing sports are great ways to elevate natural energy levels, reduce stress, improve your mood, and strengthen the body.

Why Haven't Diet Pills and Diets Worked?

Most diet pills are little more than concoctions of caffeine and other stimulants including green tea, yerba mate, ephedra, yohimbine hcl, and others. While it is possible to increase the metabolism by consuming stimulants, this is a very short lived gain. Since stimulants signal a stress response in the body, these products also increase the production of Cortisol. High amounts of Cortisol will lower the output of the thyroid gland, which is responsible for your metabolism and energy (fat) management. By temporarily increasing your metabolism with the 'help' of these diet pills, you are actually damaging your foundation for natural weight loss.

As you continue to take such a product for days or weeks, your body starts to actually store fat to prepare itself for the increased stress. What you end up with is short-lived results. And once you stop taking the diet pill, your thyroid and metabolism are running as slow as possible to save energy. With a slow metabolism, high Cortisol levels, and possible Insulin resistance, you may easily pack on more weight as you rebound from the diet pill.

Many diets fail for similar reasons. If you already suffer from the effects of Adrenal Fatigue, then your body is lacking the tools to properly burn fat.

You Are What You Eat

Now, it's no surprise that people get weary when the word 'diet' comes into play, but you truly are what you eat. Diet is one of the most important aspects in our lives, and it also plays a significant role in Adrenal Health. Nutrient deficiencies, which can easily result from a diet rich in over-processed foods, can cause significant stress on the Adrenal System.

The goal here isn't to chastise the food industry, but to shed light on how you can avoid the pitfalls in the modern-day American diet. As a consumer, you have the right to choose the foods you eat. With ingredients posted on every label, it's your responsibility to choose the ingredients that you may avoid.

One of the biggest threats to the Adrenal System has been from High Fructose Corn Syrup (HFCS) and other adulterated forms of sugar sneaking into the vast majority of the foods on the shelf. From breads to pickles, many companies have added HFCS to their products to reduce manufacturing costs and increase the flavor. While foods with HFCS are allowed to be labeled as "All-Natural", this ingredient is laboratory manufactured from corn through extensive processing.

Many of today's 'fast' and processed foods are generally high in simple sugars (refined sugar) and HFCS. The problem being that refined sugar leads to an increased Insulin release as the body reacts to the sugar and tries to store it.

Since cortisol and insulin are antagonists of one another, when you increase one of these, the other rises to control the spike. By increasing insulin from carbohydrate-rich foods, the stress hormone, cortisol, is released from the Adrenal Glands to attempt to control the insulin spike. So, just as your lifestyle, stress, and stimulants can place a toll on your Adrenal Glands, food can as well. Since highly-processed foods and fast-foods are typically high in simple sugars, this equates to a greater insulin release, which then signals the Adrenal Glands to work harder.

How can you tell good foods from bad foods?

Many people count calories and take a close look at the labels on their foods, but do you actually know what a calorie is?

A calorie is a unit of measurement, namely the unit that we use to measure the amount of energy that a food has. 'We' count calories usually by the number that is stamped on the label of most food products. But what does this number really mean?

A calorie is simply a unit of energy. Since humans use food for energy, calories are the fuel for our bodies. People all-too-often think that calories are bad for us, but we need them to survive. Weight gain and other issues are a result of simply eating too many calories each day. While your body does burn calories every second of every day, this process is amplified through exercise and increased movement. When you eat more than you can burn, the body stores the excess as fat.

So, why is this important to Adrenal Health?

Food is the fuel for our bodies. If you put contaminated fuel in your car, you'll be lucky to even get it started. Looking around the supermarket or driving down Main Street, it's easy to see that many processed foods have found their way into our supermarkets and daily diets. Many of these foods have been manufactured to serve for convenience. They can be microwaved or picked up from a drive-through and ready to eat within minutes; often they have desirable flavors that would take the average person hours to prepare. Along with flavor and convenience, few people would be willing to pay more than a few dollars per meal. All of these factors create problems, many of these processed foods and fast-foods lack a variety of vitamins and nutrients that are vital to a properly functioning body.

Antioxidants are another element that can be severely lacking in many processed foods. Foods that are rich in antioxidants include: blueberries, cranberries, apples, plums, black beans, pecans, spinach, sweet potatoes, broccoli, and many more. Your body is in a constant cycle of cellular renewal. Depending on a cell's function within the body, the life of a cell may vary from a few days (i.e. the cells in your stomach reproduce themselves quickly), to a few weeks or even months (a red blood cell lives for about 120 days). During a cell's normal daily functioning (further amplified by illness), the body creates 'free radicals'. Free radicals can be important in the body's response to illness as they are able to bind to damaged cells and help neutralize viruses and bacteria. But, free radical production is also amplified by radiation, pollution, cigarette smoke, and contact with some chemicals. Antioxidants play a particular role in this system as they have the ability to bind to free radicals, rendering them useless. Failing to consume natural foods that are rich in nutrients leaves us open to disease and illness and other stressors.

Let's place two meals side by side for comparison purposes. The double cheeseburger, medium French-fries, and medium diet soda from the local fast food restaurant, versus a chicken breast, broccoli, and a small salad with a vinegar based dressing, with a glass of water. Each costs roughly the same amount of money, yet the value of each meal to the body is entirely different. One meal is valuable to your body, the other is a liability.

The double cheeseburger meal contains over 1000 calories, which for many of you, is already 50% - 80% of the calories that you should consume in the entire day. This meal also has over 60g of fat (about 96% your daily requirement); over 1600mg of sodium; 87g of carbohydrates (about 29% your daily requirement); and 52g of protein.

On the other hand, the second meal contains approximately 350 calories, which is about the recommended size of one meal. This meal has about 7g of fat, 11g of carbohydrates, and 56g of protein. It also contains about half of the sodium.

As you can see in the chart below, the chicken meal is also high in Vitamin-C and Vitamin-E, which are potent antioxidants.

When you consume many 'fast-foods', you provide yourself with an overabundance of calories, typically exponentially higher in fat / saturated fat / Trans fat content. Since most of these foods tend to

Daily Values	Cheeseburger Meal	Chicken Meal
Calories	1000	350
Fat	60g	7g
Carbohydrates	87g	11g
Protein	52g	56g
Sodium	1600mg	740mg
Vitamin A	5%	57%
Vitamin E	10%	30%
Vitamin C	20%	165%
Vitamin B-6	59%	99%
		(All Values Appx.)

be over-processed and rely on fats and carbohydrate sources to be filling, there is little to offer in vitamins, minerals, antioxidants, and other nutrients that your body requires.

It's already been mentioned that excessive calories in your diet lead to fat and weight gain. The reason for this is that the only way your body can shed calories is by burning them. Every hour of the day, your body burns calories to provide fuel for your body and sustain your weight. When you exercise, your body is forced to work harder, which requires more energy to be output, which causes the body to use stored calories for fuel. But when you eat too many calories, and fail to burn them off throughout the day, the extra is stored as fat.

So, the fat in food is the bad guy, right? Absolutely not. While the type of calories we consume is somewhat important, the number of calories is the most important factor. Fat gets the worst reputation for a few reasons. First, most of us associate the fat around our midsection with the fat in our foods. Second, fat does contain more calories than carbohydrates or protein.

While many of us curse body fat since it seems to only stretch out our clothes, thousands of years ago fat was a key tool in the body's ability to survive during days, even weeks of famish. Without the ability to store energy as fat, humans would not have been unable to survive or grow as a race.

The fat around your midsection is not entirely linked to the fats in your food. Eating too much fat each day will lead to weight gain, but eating too much carbohydrates or protein can do the same thing. Fat is more likely to be stored in the body, as it takes far less energy to store a molecule of fat than it does a protein or carbohydrate molecule, but you NEED fat in your diet, but there are vast differences between healthy fats, and unhealthy fats.

Unhealthy fats (saturated / trans fats) are solid at room temperature and found in animal products (meat, dairy, eggs, and seafood) and some plants (coconut oil). Trans fats are not found naturally, as they are formed by the process of hydrogenating oils to increase their shelf life and boiling point. Trans fats are typically used in restaurants and processed foods as they are cheaper and keep foods from spoiling sooner. Saturated fats do have value as they aid in hormone production and assist with levels of cell production; however, most

American's tend to consume far beyond the recommended amount, leading to increased cholesterol levels and other health issues.

Healthy fats are found naturally in many foods, and are those that are liquids at room temperature. These fats are characterized into Monounsaturated and Polyunsaturated Fats. Monounsaturated fats can help to lower your 'bad' cholesterol levels as well as raise 'good' cholesterol levels. Such fats are olive oil, canola oil, and the oil from most nuts. For example, if you ever see a jar of natural peanut butter at the grocery store, there is always a layer of oil at the top of the jar, which is the natural separation of the peanut's oil from the rest of the product. Polyunsaturated fats are derived from corn, sunflowers, soy, and some seafoods such as salmon. The Omega 3 fats belong to this group of fats.

Eating healthy is not terribly difficult. As you may have fallen into the habit of eating poorly due to routine and other habits, it's easy to eat better once you get into the habit of doing so. The key is moderation. Many people fear they will suffer cravings for sugar as well as heavily-salted treats. The trick is to make gradual changes every week. If you normally eat a 12 inch sandwich for lunch, try ¾ of a sandwich and save the other portion for later. Restaurants are often culprit to your diet because many offer servings that are three and four times the recommended portion. Get in the habit of taking at least half of your meals home, and save it for a later meal.

It is important to understand how eating patterns affect your adrenal health. As mentioned before, your body is always trying to maintain a state of homeostasis, or stability. The less stressors that impact the body, the easier this process is. When you eat a meal that is high in calories or refined sugars, the body has to perform complex chemical processes in order to combat the unneeded sugars, and regain stability.

With the advent of low-carb diets, many people chastised all carbohydrates without understanding the good from the bad. Just as there are healthy and unhealthy fats, there are healthy and unhealthy carbohydrates. Healthy carbohydrates are full of fiber and typically rich in vitamins, minerals, and antioxidants. Unhealthy carbohydrates are foods that are heavily sugared.

It might surprise you to learn that the sugar cravings that you often experience are the result of a previous heavily sugared meal or snack. With every meal you eat, a chemical called insulin is released, which aids the body in the absorption of sugar (glucose) and signals the body to turn off the feeling of hunger. After this signal spikes, you are left feeling satisfied for a few hours, but the insulin signal is influenced by the amount of sugars in the meal. When you consume a meal that is comprised of simple sugars (i.e. pancakes, white breads, baked potato, many cereals), these foods are broken down very quickly, leading to a sudden release of glucose into the body. High insulin levels can also increase weight gain since they signal glucose to be stored in the cells.

Healthy carbohydrates, on the other hand, take more time to break down. These foods, such as whole-grains, some pasta, fruits, vegetables, and bran cereals, release their glucose over a longer period of time. This allows the body to remain in a state of homeostasis, avoiding the often 'crash' after a sugary meal. Since these foods release their sugars over a longer period of time, the body can sustain energy at a regular rate.

The unhealthy carbohydrate foods are metabolized much quicker, often leading to the quick elimination of glucose and into a sudden state of fatigue and drowsiness two to three hours after the meal. Typically, this 'crash' is also accompanied by cravings for more sugary foods, as the body attempts to overcompensate for the sudden drop in blood sugar levels.

The Birth of Cylapril

With a little better understanding of the Adrenal system, how stress affects your body, and how diet and lifestyle play a significant role in your Adrenal health, it's important to explain how the Cylapril Adrenal Weight Loss System can help you manage your stress.

Our first course of action in developing a formula to provide relief for Adrenal Fatigue was to first identify what Adrenal Fatigue was, what caused it, and how it affected the body. One of the main problems with researching Adrenal Fatigue is that much of the medical industry has yet to identify it as a documented health concern. There are millions of people that suffer from Adrenal Fatigue symptoms, but many doctors don't know how to identify Adrenal disorders until the patient shows signs of Addison's disease, Cushing's Syndrome, or another 'textbook' illness. While there are tests that identify Adrenal Fatigue, unless your doctor is familiar with Adrenal Fatigue, it is possible that your symptoms will be passed on as another issue.

In order for an effective Adrenal Fatigue product to work, it must do two things: assist in the revitalization of the Adrenal Glands, and help reduce the amount of stress that the body faces. Using this dual approach allows the body the best opportunity to prevent further damage to the Adrenal Glands while restoring energy as well as functionality. While relief can be present within days, repairing years of damage can take weeks to months depending on each person's particular situation.

The first formula of the Cylapril system is the Cylapril Adrenal Fatigue Regulator. This formula works directly with the adrenal system to provide it with the nutrients that are often lacking when Adrenal Fatigue is present. By directly supplementing the Adrenal Glands, for the first time since your last 'true' vacation, they are not forced to work at exhausting rates to provide you with the energy that you demand. Cylapril also works directly with the stimulants that you consume.

Cylapril is the first product designed to specifically lessen your dependency to stimulants by counteracting the buffering that occurs on your A1 and A2 receptors from abusing stimulants like caffeine, ephedra, amphetamines and nicotine. As mentioned earlier, A1 and A2 receptors are essential to your health because they regulate your natural energy levels.

The second part of the Cylapril System is the Cylapril Anti Stress & Energy Revitalizer. One of the most effective methods of reducing the stress that the Adrenal Glands suffer is to reduce the amount of stress that your body needs to adjust to daily. This formula utilizes several natural ingredients that work together to enable your body to react less dramatically to minor daily stressors. By relieving the stress that you face constantly, you should find yourself in a better, more positive mood, and you should find your days full of more energy.

One of the most important aspects of this system is that it is entirely stimulant free; there is no caffeine or other energizers that would only mask your symptoms, yet never correct them. The Anti-Stress and Energy Revitalizer helps to increase your natural energy without adding to the damaging stress that stimulants are responsible for.

The Cylapril Adrenal Weight Loss-System

The Cylapril Adrenal Weight Loss System differs from many other approaches to fatigue management and Weight loss in that it treats the problem, rather than simply masking the symptoms with stimulants. Many people who suffer various fatigue symptoms are often prescribed stimulants and prescription amphetamines. Rather than treating the causes of the fatigue, these approaches simply mask the fatigue by forcing the Adrenal Glands to produce more energy. Many prescription amphetamines are also much more potent than caffeine and the more common over-the-counter stimulants that we consume each day. While these products will provide a quick fix, they can just as easily cause some symptoms to worsen as the Adrenal Glands are pushed into overdrive. What you end up with is a temporary solution, but a much more serious problem down the line.

Another factor in which the Cylapril Adrenal Weight Loss System differs from many is through actual testing and customer feedback. While anyone can read a few reports and clinical studies and base a product around this, this does not guarantee something that will be effective in the real world. There are thousands of peer reviewed articles, studies, and trials of various natural ingredients, but just because something is effective in controlled studies does not guarantee that the average person will have the same success. While Cylapril was based on certain published double-blind placebo controlled studies, it also has proven itself within the real world and the real person's lifestyle. Over the past few years, we have tested over ten formulas as we worked towards a 360-degree approach for restoring adrenal function. We had great success with each of these formulas, but one in particular gave us the user success that we were looking for. This formula was unique in that it was formulated with bodybuilders and performance athletes in mind. The difference from a performance athlete from the average person is the amount of physical stress that the body endures from this sport. While physical and emotional stress is almost worlds apart in their cause, they have very similar and potent effects on the body. Furthermore, many performance athletes consume hundreds, if not thousands of milligrams of caffeine and other stimulants per day in order to energize themselves and ensure that they can push their physical limits each day, which is the only way to grow in strength.

Another major difference separating many performance athletes from the average person is the diet and foods that we consume. Athletes are most likely to consume foods that are rich in vitamins, minerals, antioxidants, and other essential compounds. Also many follow strict dietary guidelines that are rich in protein and complex carbohydrates, yet avoid the unhealthy fat categories. Furthermore, exercising is a great stress reliever, which reverts us back to the basis of our previous conclusion: athletes suffer from many physical stressors, but many don't necessarily face the same emotional stressors; while all face emotional stressors, athletes are provided significant relief through their sport.

Our goal was to formulate a product that would be equally effective for everyone, but in order to do this we had to formulate a product that would be equally effective for people facing physical stress, emotional stress, and those who faced both.

While we cannot make someone into an athlete, we can supplement the average person to give them some of the advantages that athletes have. This became the birth of a two-part system. We felt that only using a one-approach system severely limited the type of people that Cylapril would be effective for.

Formula One of the Cylapril System, the Adrenal Fatigue Regulator, has shown to be extremely effective for nearly everyone who tested it. It is responsible for revitalizing the Adrenal Glands, supplementing necessary nutrients, and breaking your tolerance and resistance to stimulants.

Formula Two of the Cylapril System, the Anti Stress and Energy Revitalizer, is what helps alleviate emotional stress from the average person by supplying necessary nutrients such as a potent antioxidant and Vitamins A, B, C, D, and E. In addition, this formula has been shown to have a positive effect on depression, anxiety, and immune function. Most importantly, this formula helps to cut some of the impact that stress taxes on the body, allowing you greater physical and mental performance while naturally reducing fatigue and the stress-reaction. Again, both of these formulas are completely stimulant-free.

It's also important to note that both formulas of Cylapril are free of depressants. While it is somewhat common in the medical field to provide stressed and anxiety patients with central nervous system depressants to help them 'feel' less stressed, all this often does is make the person 'aware' of less. Typically, such medicines will cause drowsiness, impaired motor function, and even depression. I don't know about you, but the last thing I need to get me through a busy day is a sedative!

How Does Cylapril Work?

To understand the Cylapril Adrenal Weight loss System, it is important to understand how the key elements in Cylapril aid in the relief and repair of your Adrenal Fatigue. We have highlighted some of the ingredients to help you understand how this revolutionary system

Formula 1:
Cylapril Adrenal Fatigue Regulator

Pantothenic Acid

Pantothenic acid is one of the key components in helping promote adrenal health. Once inside the body, pantothenic acid forms a substance called pantethine, which is further converted into an enzyme called "Co-enzyme A." Co-enzyme A is an extremely important compound and is essential in the metabolism of protein, fat, and carbohydrates. It is also the starting point for the body's production of adrenal steroids, cholesterol, bile, and haemoglobin. Pantethine allows the adrenal glands to generate more cortisone, which is an anti-stress hormone. With more cortisone produced, the body's inflammatory response is reduced. The increased production of cortisone and other adrenal hormones stimulated by Pantothenic acid helps counteract stress and enhance metabolism.

Schizandra

Schizandra is a recognized adaptogen, capable of increasing the body's ability to resist both disease and stress. Scientific studies demonstrate Schizandra's ability to increase work capacity, exercise capacity, mental capacity, and adaptability to darkness and other environmental stresses in both animal and human studies. While alleviating stress and fighting fatigue, Schizandra has been shown to help improve the overall health of the adrenals.

Thiamin (Vitamin B1)

Thiamin, a water-soluble vitamin, exits the body daily so it must be taken on a regular basis. Thiamin is essential in processing of carbohydrates, fat, and protein. Every cell of the body requires thiamin to form adenosine triphosphate (ATP), which is an energy-carrying molecule found in the cells of all living things. Studies show that thiamin is directly associated with helping the body to manage stress. Thiamine also assists in blood formation, carbohydrate metabolism, and the production of hydrochloric acid, which is important for proper digestion.

Passion Flower Extract

Passion flower has demonstrated an ability to relieve stress and anxiety while also working to relieve fatigue. In a double blind study conducted in 2001, 18 patients who were given Passion flower showed an improvement for general anxiety disorder.

Passion flower has a sedative and antispasmodic action, and this relaxes spasms and tension in one's muscles. These actions in turn calms the nerves and also lessens anxiety, tensions, and any other type of physical pain that is closely associated with stress and high blood pressure.

Licorice Root

Licorice Root helps to reduce the amount of hydrocortisone broken down by the liver, thereby reducing the workload of the Adrenal Glands. Licorice quickly tones the adrenals by relaxing and strengthening them to continue pumping out adrenaline, but in more calculated amounts. Licorice has been found to have a very beneficial and nourishing effect on the Adrenal Glands as long as some portion of the gland is healthy. Addison's disease, which decreases adrenal cortex secretions, has been treated with success with licorice extracts. Licorice is known to stimulate the production of the cortin hormone, which is useful when the body is under mental and emotional stress and helps with the coping process.

Adrenal Ext, Bovine

Bovine Adrenal Ext. is particularly important in the initial phases of adrenal repair since it provides raw materials to support adrenal function. It also contains some vital adrenal chemical-messengers that are lacking in human body when you are in a state of adrenal fatigue. By including Adrenal Tissue it relieves the adrenal glands' burden and allows the following to occur:

- Relief from the major symptoms of poorly functioning adrenals much sooner than waiting for the adrenals to become healthy again – a process that can take weeks or months.
- Significantly faster adrenal recovery leading to increased energy

Biotin

Biotin is a B vitamin that plays an extremely important role in energy metabolism and function. It has been shown to help essential enzymes break down carbohydrates, fats, and proteins.

Panax Ginseng Powder

Panax Ginseng is best known as an adaptogen, which is a substance that may help individuals deal with physical and emotional stress.

Another common use for Panax ginseng is for its ability to bolster the immune system.

Jujube Extract

Jujube acts as an adaptogen by encouraging normal functioning of the adrenal glands, allowing the adrenal glands to function optimally when challenged by stress. Jujube has been shown to enhance mental acuity and physical endurance without the crash that often comes from caffeine.

Riboflavin (vitamin B2)

Riboflavin, along with the other B vitamins, supports energy production/transfer by aiding in the metabolizing of fats, carbohydrates, and proteins. Riboflavin is also needed for red blood cell formation and respiration, antibody production, and for regulating human growth and reproduction. Riboflavin is an essential nutrient in basic nutrition for humans and plays a vital role in the production of energy. Riboflavin is needed to process and break down amino acids and fats, activate vitamin B6 and folic acid, and help convert carbohydrates into ATP - the fuel the body runs on. Like vitamin B1 (thiamine), riboflavin plays a crucial role in basic metabolic reactions, chiefly the conversion of carbohydrates into sugar, which is used by the body to produce energy. Thiamine and riboflavin promote the first steps in the metabolism (breakdown and production) of glucose (sugar) and of fatty acids.

Manganese Ascorbate

Maganese aids in the formation of connective tissue, bones, blood-clotting factors, and sex hormones, and it plays a role in fat and carbohydrate metabolism (energy production), calcium absorption, and blood sugar regulation. Manganese is also helpful for normal brain and proper nerve function. Ascorbate better known as Vitamin C helps normalize stress-hormone levels. Optimal amounts of Ascorbate (Vitamin C) help keep the body from fatiguing. Fatigue and easy bruising is an early warning sign of Vitamin C deficiency.

5-HTP

5-HTP (5-Hydroxytryptophan) is a naturally-occurring amino acid and is a precursor to the neurotransmitter serotonin. Serotonin is believed to play an important role as a neurotransmitter, in the regulation of anger, aggression, body temperature, mood, sleep, sexuality, and appetite. In certain circles serotonin is referred to as the happy amino acid. The lifestyle and dietary followings of many people living in this stress-filled day and age can result in lowered levels of serotonin within the brain.

Zinc Ascorbate

Zinc plays important roles in bone growth, maintaining healthy skin and bones, metabolic processes, and it is essential for the synthesis and metabolism of proteins. Zinc also has been shown to help provide your body with optimal immune system support. Ascorbate better known as Vitamin C (and previously discussed in maganese ascorbate) helps normalize stress-hormone levels. Optimal amounts of Ascorbate (Vitamin C) help keep the body from fatiguing.

Formula Two:
Cylapril Anti Stress & Energy Revitalizing Formula

Bee Pollen Powder

Bee pollen is often referred to as nature's most complete source of food. Bee pollen's benefits has been praised and talked about in books and even the Bible, other religious books, and ancient Chinese and Egyptian texts. It has high concentrations of the B -vitamin complex, and also contains Vitamins A, C, D, and E. Bee Pollen has demonstrated weight control benefits which include improving your metabolism, and to the high percentage of lecithin contained in bee pollen, it improves lipolysis, which is the breakdown of fat stored in fat cells. It may also help reduce your cravings for food.

Bee Pollen contains more than 96 different nutrients, including every single nutrient that is needed to sustain human life. It is made up of 40% protein, the majority of which is usable by the body without any further breakdown or metabolism. Bee pollen combines 22 amino acids, vitamin C, B-complex and folic acid, polyunsaturated fatty acids, enzymes, and carotene, calcium, magnesium, selenium, nucleic acids, lecithin, and cysteine.

Ashwagandha Powder
Ashwagandha improves the body's ability to maintain physical effort and helps the body cope with stress. Ashwagandha herb promotes sound sleep, reduces anxiety and stress, and improves immune function and mood. Ashwagandha is an adaptogen, and it also acts to restore hypothalamic and peripheral receptor sensitivity to the effects of cortisol and other adrenal hormones. It is through this method that adaptogens enable the body to mount an appropriate stress response with lower amounts of cortisol than would otherwise be required.

Rhodiola Rosea

Rhodiola Rosea has been shown to be quite effective for improving mood, alleviating depression and fatigue. Clinical research shows that it improves both physical and mental performance, and reduces fatigue. Rhodiola Rosea's mood enhancing effects are attributed to its ability to optimize serotonin and dopamine levels. It also improves your adrenal gland reserves.

How to Take the Cylapril
Adrenal Weight-Loss System

The exact timing and other minor particulars of how you take the Cylapril Adrenal Weight loss System will make little difference in its effectiveness. This product will have the same effectiveness whether or not you take it with or without food. There would not be any side effects, or contradictions when taking this product with or without meals. Since some of the ingredients are rich in water-soluble vitamins such as Vitamins A, C, D, and E, we advised that you take Cylapril with at least 4-8 oz of water, as this will increase their absorption.

The most common question we are asked is "Do I have to stop drinking coffee while I take Cylapril?"

Absolutely not. While the body will be able to repair itself at the greatest pace without the presence of caffeine and other stimulants in the blood-stream, this is impossible for many people to even think of. One of the side-effects that result from excessive stimulant use is that the body eventually forms a physical addiction to stimulants. For people with stimulant addictions, it would be somewhat painful (severe headache, irritability), and very inconvenient for many people to give up caffeine in its entirety.

If you are able to avoid caffeine on a daily basis, you will be doing the most justice to your body and giving it the best environment for a swift recovery. If this is not an option, than it is important to try to only use the least amount of stimulants that you can. Rather than ordering a large coffee, double espresso, or large diet soda, aim for a smaller portion. If you cannot do this on the first day, slowly cut back your intake a little more each day. Depending on your current situation, breaking your addiction to caffeine can take a few days, or a few weeks.

Nearly everyone who has provided us feedback after taking Cylapril has mentioned the fact that they were able to consume fewer stimulants, yet still get a potent punch from this lower dose. For most people, this means that within as little as two weeks, ½ your usual cup of coffee (or ½ your stimulant of choice) will be enough to deliver the energy that you were use to before Cylapril. This is one of the signs that the Cylapril system is working very effectively for you. For those of you who consume the canned energy drinks available at the gas stations that sell at close to $3 a can, this can mean big savings! Many people have been amazed to find that in many cases, the Cylapril system will pay for itself in the first month alone. Just think about how much you spend each month in coffee, energy drinks, or diet pills; many people spend up to $5 to $10 a day on these.

Many people ask if both formulas, the Adrenal Fatigue Regulator and the Anti-Stress and Energy Revitalizer, can be taken at the same time. This is definitely acceptable and will not hurt the effectiveness of either product. If you would rather take them at different times, you may do so as well. The exact timing of these products is not as important as is getting them into your system daily. With daily use, the system is able to give you the best results. If you do happen to miss a dose or even an entire day, just take the next dose at your regularly scheduled time; there is no need or even benefit from doubling the dose.

Most people will find that 2 capsules daily of each formula will be an effective dose. If you do not see results within the first day or two, this does not mean that you need a higher dose. For most of us, the relief will be experienced at first within the first week, with the benefits improving more and more each week.

The maximum dose of 3 capsules daily (of each system) is recommended for persons who have a physical addiction to caffeine or other stimulants. This means that you cannot function without stimulants in your system and/or you consume an unusually high amount of coffee or other stimulants (including nicotine from cigarettes) each day. Most people who fall into this category are those who experience a significant headache unless their stimulant of choice is consumed.

To give you a better understanding of how to take Cylapril and what to expect, we have illustrated the three common lifestyles of people who take Cylapril. To find which Scenario you fit into, just see which one best fits your day. This will help you to understand the dose, what to expect, and when to expect it.

Scenario One (Minor Adrenal Fatigue)

- Mild to moderate caffeine / nicotine / other stimulant use
- Mildly stressful life
- Trouble getting out of bed
- Fatigue in early-morning and mid-afternoon
- Most productive in the evening
- Weight gain
- Sugar / salt cravings

People in this category may suffer Adrenal symptoms mostly caused by stress. If you are in this category of fatigue, you generally consume a below average amount of coffee and/or nicotine on a daily basis. You might drink 1-2 cups of coffee or another caffeinated beverage per day (or smoke less than a few cigarettes); typically, a small cup of coffee in the morning and maybe a caffeinated soda around lunch. You don't need caffeine to operate and can get by fine without any caffeine in your system for at least 48 hours straight if needed.

At this point, you might be over-worked at your job, or face other stressors due to your home life or even school. I mention school because for many of us, college was where we started to consume caffeine for the sole reason of energy. This was the beginning of our stimulant abuse and stressful days.

You should not feel entirely exhausted at this point. Perhaps drowsy and unmotivated to get out of bed in the morning, no matter what time you try to get up. You are probably somewhat fatigued during the mid-afternoon and you may have decreased mental capacity and a loss of concentration. Most likely you have the greatest amount of sustained energy as well as the best productivity in the early to late evening.

What you need to do:
At this point, minor changes are necessary to ensure that your symptoms do not worsen, but it is vital to make these changes before a minor problem turns into a significant health concern. Usually at this stage, a short break in the afternoon consisting of relaxing with a book or a 15-minute power nap is often enough to settle the nerves and aid the body in relaxation. You should also take diet and exercise into consideration; this will allow your body to perform at its greatest capacity.

What to expect with Cylapril:

Month One – Initial Relief and Initial Repair
- General relief from stress
- Increased energy, mental focus, and memory
- Increased mood / sense of well being

- Easier to get out of bed
- More motivation
- Notice an improved metabolism
- Initial stages of Adrenal revitalization

Month Two – Relief and Energy Rejuvenation
- Increased endurance
- Better ability to lose weight
- Continued revitalization of adrenal function
- More natural balance of stress hormones
- Natural energy begins to increase

Months Three through Six – Optimal Function and Energy
- Optimal Adrenal function
- Greatest ability to lose stress-induced weight
- Sustained natural energy
- Improved Sleep and Moods

Since you are likely to have minimal damage to your adrenal glands at this point, the program is effective in the least amount of time. For this scenario, you will most likely see results within the first 2-4 days of taking Cylapril.

The first effects to be noticed are the ability to handle mid-afternoon tasks without fatiguing as intensely. As a whole, you should be able to handle stress more efficiently and often have more patience with minor stressors. Within the first week of Cylapril, most people mention that it is much easier to get out of bed, and they are less likely to hit snooze a few extra times.

The length of time that you remain on the Cylapril Adrenal Weight Loss System will vary from person to person. The above schedule is just a general guide to which most will see the intended results. It is important to note that your health and lifestyle is entirely in your control, your results may vary depending on your diet, lifestyle, and other factors.

Since most people with mild Adrenal Fatigue have the lease amount of damage to their Adrenals, Cylapril may be taken for 2 – 6 months depending on your preference and relief from fatigue. It can be taken longer should you wish to continue to supplement your Adrenal system and assist your day with stress relief and efficient adrenal functioning.

Scenario Two (Significant Adrenal Fatigue)

- Medium to moderate caffeine / nicotine / other stimulant use
- Typically need caffeine to 'wake-up' in the morning
- Physical / emotional stressors are very common daily if not endless
- Constant fatigue throughout the day
- Weight gain
- Mild to moderate depression
- Sleep disorders
- Sugar / salt cravings
- Lack of motivation including decreased sex drive

People in this category suffer from stress as a likely combination of stress, poor lifestyle habits (including diet and lack of exercise), mild / moderately excessive caffeine use, and other factors. Your lifestyle might not include every cause just mentioned, but you can probably identify with at least 2 – 4 of these factors. For the most part, Adrenal Fatigue is always caused by more than one source; many varied stressors can place a similar, yet significant toll on the Adrenal Glands.

In this category, you are more likely to need a cup of coffee or another stimulant in the morning. You are able to get out of bed, but with significant difficulty. On most mornings, you don't seem to wake up until you get your morning cup of coffee. For some of you, it may be possible to get by without one, but you probably don't either function too crisply, or can't seem to fully wake up without it.

You are likely to work a full time job, and often balance numerous obligations or stressors outside of the workplace: children, debt, errands, and marital issues.

At this point, you may feel like you have entered an almost perpetual state of fatigue and stress. You might have the energy needed to get through the day, but are more likely to find yourself dozing-off while watching television in the early evening. The thought of exercising after work may seem like a great idea, but by the time you get out of work, you are too exhausted. Eating a healthy dinner probably seems like a great idea, but it's just too convenient to pick up a prepared meal or eat out. Your energy reserves are mostly extinguished by the time you leave work, so you make it home in attempts to relax and deal with the almost-daily emotional stressors of home. Despite all of this fatigue, you probably have not had a refreshing night's sleep in some time. Many people in this category suffer from some sort of sleep disorder, whether it is trouble falling asleep, or problems sleeping entirely through the night.

What you need to do:
At this point, some significant changes should be taken into consideration to both repair the damage to the Adrenal System, and prevent further damage that could escalate into a worsening condition.

In order to fully reverse the damage that has taken place, you must identify the lifestyle factors that are contributing the most to your physical and emotional stress, and consider ways to alleviate their effects on your body.

I recommended that you take a minimum of a 15-minute break at some point in the early to mid-afternoon. This break should avoid all stressors and can be something as easy as a slow-paced walk outside, preferably away from people, vehicle traffic, or other obnoxious distractions. Many people benefit greatly from meditating or utilizing another psychological relaxation method. If the location or weather does not permit for this, even sitting in your car will allow you to escape the pressure of your job. Close your eyes and clear your mind of stress, errands, and other obstructions. It might not be a bad idea to set an alarm clock on your cell phone for this in case you happen to doze off during this. It's one less thing to worry about.

Another great way to alleviate stress is to write it down. We often have sleep disorders because our mind is utilizing the time when we sleep to try to categorize errands and other tasks. Each night, write down a list of the things you need to do the next day, and even the next week if you have a deadline or another obligation. It's an even better idea to get a small notebook and use it each day to write down thoughts, ideas, to-do lists, etc. This will help you stay organized as well as allow your brain to focus on your intended task, rather than your grocery list.

You should also take your diet and exercise into consideration. Even a jog or brisk walk outside or 20 minutes on a treadmill is enough to boost the natural energy stores and help your overall health. Making gradual changes in both exercise and diet will help you to stick to a healthier lifestyle for a longer period of time. In regards to diet, try to include more fresh foods such as fresh vegetables, fruit, and unprocessed meats. Many nutritionists and dieticians recommend that if a food label has more than 5 ingredients on it, than it is probably over-processed.

What to expect with Cylapril:

Months One and Two – Relief
- General relief from stress
- Increased energy
- Increased mental focus and memory
- Increased mood / sense of well-being
- Easier to get out of bed
- Notice an improved metabolism
- More energy from your 'normal' dose of stimulants / caffeine

Months Two through Four – Relief and Energy Rejuvenation
- Increased physical endurance
- Better ability to lose weight
- Initial stages of Adrenal revitalization
- Enhanced mood and improved patience

Months Five through Nine – Optimal Function and Energy
- Optimal Adrenal Revitalization
- Greatest ability to lose stress-induced weight
- Restored Natural Energy levels

Many of you will start to notice the effects of Cylapril within the first week; most will see some results in the first day or two. Typically, within this time you will notice a significant boost in clear, natural energy in the afternoons. Your mood will not sway as dramatically throughout the day, and you may not become as irritable over minor stressors and hassles.

Within a week or two, most people find themselves free from their tolerance and dependence on caffeine and they can operate with either much less, or none at all. With each week, it is important to lower the dose of stimulants that you consume; this will increase the progress of Adrenal Repair and start you off on a healthier lifestyle.

For complete relief from Adrenal Fatigue, the process can take from two or three months, to a complete year. While it can be disconcerting to think that relief can take up to 12 months, most people report that they have greatly renewed source of energy within the first month or two. While your energy stores will return quickly with the help of the Cylapril system, it will take some time before the Adrenal Glands are restored to proper function. And, now that you are finally aware of the habits and lifestyle factors that play a major role in causing Adrenal Fatigue, it will be that much easier to live a lifestyle more conducive to adrenal health.

The length of time that you remain on the Cylapril Adrenal Weight-Loss System will vary from person to person. The above schedule is just a general guide to which most will see the intended results. It is important to note that your health and lifestyle is entirely in your control, your results may vary depending on your diet, lifestyle, and other factors.

Since most people with moderate Adrenal Fatigue have a significant amount of damage to their Adrenals, Cylapril may be taken for 4 – 9 months depending on your preference and relief from fatigue. It can be taken longer should you wish to continue to supplement your Adrenal system and assist your day with stress relief and efficient adrenal functioning.

Scenario Three (Adrenal Exhaustion)

- Excessive caffeine / nicotine / other stimulant use (abuse)
- You 'need' caffeine / stimulants to function
- Extremely stressful / extremely demanding job
- Extreme / chronic fatigue (may be masked by constant stimulant use)
- Performance and mental abilities suffer
- Excessive weight gain
- Poor diet & lack of exercise
- Mild to severe depression symptoms
- Chronic sleep disorders
- Significant lack of motivation
- Moderate to excessive drop in sex drive
- Loss of physical strength

People in this category are most likely to face Adrenal disorders due to a combination of several significant factors. Years of stimulant abuse, lack of sleep, and/or poor diet and lifestyle choices have taxed the life out of your Adrenal Glands. Most people in this category have developed a pear-shaped body type due to the excessive amounts of insulin and cortisol that are secreted on a daily basis.

If you fit into this category, you may have some sort of addiction to stimulants, whether caffeine or nicotine, you find it almost impossible to function without a potent dose of your stimulant of choice. Typically, you consume a steady flow of coffee or energy drinks throughout the entire day. I've even spoken to some people who consume well over 1,000 mg's of caffeine per day! With the average cup of fresh brewed coffee containing around 80 – 100mg of caffeine, these levels become rather dangerous when you take the list of associated side effects into account.

At this point, you are likely to feel that you are in a perpetual state of fatigue. While it is possible to reach this level without the use of stimulants, it would require a significantly stressful lifestyle with little or no time for relaxation other than sleep. Generally, you probably feel run-down at most time of the day, but you continue to work and operate under stressful conditions to meet the required demand.

What you need to do:
At this level, the most important factor is slowly eliminating the factors that are causing the Adrenal stress. This will vary greatly from person to person, but will typically revolve around a combination of various stressors that are amplified by the steady flow of stimulants in the system. Many people who abuse diet pills and other thermogenics will also fit into this category. However, it is possible to reach this level of Adrenal Fatigue without regularly consuming stimulants if there is enough impact from other factors.

Since the body is able to compete with a certain amount of stress, it is important to maximize the amount of stress that you can handle in a day. Since the body only truly repairs itself when you sleep, it is vital that you allow yourself extra time for sleep and relaxation. If you typically settle down each night in-front of the television or computer, you might find better relaxation with a book or magazine. Dark and dim lights signal the release of sleep hormones in the body, causing the increased sensation of drowsiness. The bright and focused light from the television or computer monitor will often confuse the brain, and cause it to delay drowsiness for some time. Some people might disagree with this statement thinking that they have no problem falling asleep with the 'sleep' timer set, but while you can fall asleep, you are more likely to experience a decreased release of sleep hormones, leaving you with unfulfilling or unrelaxing sleep.

It's also suggested that you begin to add as many unprocessed foods as possible. Bring raw vegetables and fruits with you for snacks. Substitute French fries and side-dishes for healthier options.

If you do not get adequate exercise, it is important to add this into your lifestyle. However, at this level of fatigue, it is important to get the right type of exercise. Strenuous exercises such as heavy resistance training (bodybuilding) and/or long periods of cardio can actually ADD to the amount of stress your body faces. While such activities are recommended for persons with healthy adrenal function, your body may have a hard time recovering from overly strenuous activities. Instead, it is recommended that you engage in lighter activities: lower weight resistance training, low intensity cardio, yoga, etc. These activities will still provide the benefits of exercising, but will not compromise your recovery by adding in another significant stressor.
If you do not currently exercise, a great way to get started is by walking a mile or two a day at a brisk pace. Every few days, increase the

distance and/or your speed. This can be done in as little as 30 minutes per day and is an easy way for someone to get into exercising without investing in a gym membership or expensive cardio machines. Also, walking outside is beneficial because it is relaxing and a good de-stressor.

What to expect with Cylapril:

Months One and Two – Relief
- General relief from stress
- Increased energy
- Increased mental focus and memory
- Increased mood / sense of well-being
- Easier to get out of bed
- Notice an improved metabolism
- More energy from your 'normal' dose of stimulants / caffeine

Months Three through Six – Relief and Energy Rejuvenation
- Increased endurance
- Better ability to lose weight
- Initial stages of Adrenal revitalization
- Enhanced mood and improved patience

Months Six through Twelve – Optimal Function and Energy
- Optimal Adrenal revitalization
- Greatest ability to lose stress-induced weight
- Greatest ability to lose stress-induced weight
- Restored Natural Energy levels

Even people with extreme cases of Adrenal Fatigue have felt relief with the Cylapril Adrenal Weight Loss System in mere days. Most people will experience a relief from stress, with the greater ability to handle stress. Fatigue decreases as the person is able to achieve greater energy levels without heavy doses of stimulants.

Most will experience the relief and energizing effects of Cylapril within the first week; extreme cases can take two weeks and longer for significant relief. While you will probably feel much better through the first month of Cylapril, it is important to understand that reversing the damage of Adrenal Fatigue can take some time. In extreme cases of Adrenal Fatigue, fully repairing the Adrenal Glands can take from 6-12 months and beyond.

While it can be disconcerting to think that relief can take more than 12 months, most people report that they have a greatly renewed source of energy within the first month. While your energy stores will return quickly with the help of the Cylapril system, it will take some time before the Adrenal Glands are restored to proper function.

The length of time that you remain on the Cylapril Adrenal Weight Loss System will vary from person to person. The above schedule is just a general guide to which most will see the intended results. It is important to note that your health and lifestyle is entirely in your control, your results may vary depending on your diet, lifestyle, and other factors.

Since most people with extreme Adrenal Fatigue have a significant amount of damage to their Adrenals, Cylapril may be taken for 12 months or as long as needed based on your preference or until you establish relief from fatigue. It can be taken longer should you wish to continue to supplement your Adrenal system and assist your day with stress relief and efficient adrenal functioning.

Your Lifestyle in Recovery from Adrenal Fatigue

While Cylapril is a complete system that was formulated to give your body the absolute best opportunity to revitalize your Adrenal System, it will still take effort on your part to ensure complete repair and to maintain proper functioning through the future.

Our body's greatest tool is its power to adapt. Thousands of years ago, humans lived simpler lifestyles. Day to day activity was solely surrounded by the need to secure enough food to survive. With this simpler life, came different stressors from what we experience today. As a hunter / gatherer, man was constantly in competition with the most aggressive animals in the hunt for food. This is where our Adrenal System became valuable. Just as today, it provides a surge of energy when facing danger, thousands of years ago it was a vital tool enabling humans to fight off predators and escape dangerous situations.

The differences in lifestyle from then to now are almost inconceivable. While early man would have faced few dangers each day that would trigger adrenaline release and enhanced Adrenal function, today, we face endless sources of stress. On top of the physical stressors that we endure, we now face almost endless emotional stressors from family, money, as well as a lifestyle that doesn't promote idleness. We then further stress our bodies with poor diet choices, lack of exercise, lack of sleep, excessive abuse of stimulants, and a lifestyle often void of relaxation.

With the body's ability to adapt comes the body's ability to accept the endless stressors of today's lifestyle. The body triggers feelings of fatigue to signal us to rest. Rather than accept our limitations, we consume any one of a number of stimulants to mask fatigue and continue working. As this cycle continues, the body attempts to adapt by releasing increased number of hormones. As this process continues for days, even for months and years, the Adrenal System simply exceeds its output until it finally cannot function any further. Eventually the system becomes fatigued, hormone levels are impaired, and you begin to suffer the results of perpetual fatigue.

The key to addressing Adrenal Fatigue is to address the root of the problem: your lifestyle. Each person will have a different solution to solving this problem; just as each of us have different causes for Adrenal Fatigue.

Living an 'Ideal Lifestyle' would provide the absolute best scenario for Adrenal Repair; however, it is impractical for the majority of us. This 'Ideal Lifestyle' would be to run off to the beaches of Tahiti (or your ideal relaxing destination), and not have to work, manage your family, or deal with any monetary issues. Doesn't sound too practical, does it?

The problem is that many other recommendations for treating Adrenal Fatigue are impractical. Many of these include significant changes such as eliminating all stimulants from your diet, eliminating stress, getting to bed before 10 pm and sleeping past 9 am, and avoiding television and computers. While we do agree that this is all important for Adrenal repair, none of this is realistic for the average person. In order to restore your health, you need to identify the traits in your life that contributed to Adrenal Fatigue, and take responsibility for what you can realistically change.

Rather than demand impractical changes, we suggest altering your lifestyle to one that is more conducive to repair, allows greater time for rest and relaxation, and includes a balanced diet, and relaxing exercise. By taking small steps in the right direction, you will be able to drastically change your lifestyle without even realizing it. You don't have to change your life overnight; this can just add to your stress.

What you can do on a daily basis:

Slow your pace
Figure out what you can do to manage your time better. If money is the source of your troubles, seek counseling from a financial advisor or accountant. While speaking with a financial advisor might cost you a few dollars upfront, it will most likely pay for itself overtime.

If you normally spend a few hours watching television before bed try reading or conversing with family or friends.

Schedule your priorities for the day. Make sure you accomplish what is important, and spend less time addressing issues that may be trivial.

Write things down
One of the main causes of sleep disorders is stress that follows you to bed. Quite often, any stress that is not resolved throughout the day will cause you to have nightmares, toss and turn, wake up suddenly, and wake up unrefreshed. By making a to-do list, or jotting down the things that you are worried about, your mind can relax rather than remained focused all night.

There is no point rehearsing your grocery list or the bills that you have to pay when you should be sleeping. Write them down, take it off your mind, and enjoy your dreams.

Exercise

Some people are terrified by the word exercise. The key is finding something that you enjoy doing. Many gyms these days even have cardio machines with individual cable televisions on each machine. By pacing yourself at a comfortable speed, you may be amazed by how well you feel after 30 – 60 minutes on a treadmill, elliptical, or bicycle machine. Exercise greatly increases the body's output of endorphins, natural pain killers that are released in the body that provide euphoria or a greater sense of well-being.

Exercise is also a great tool for combating depression symptoms as well as fighting stress. When dealing with Adrenal Fatigue, the most important consideration to take into account is that your exercise is not extremely strenuous, such as long, high paced cardio sessions, or extremely heavy resistance training. Exercise does create minor physical stress on the body that must be repaired, but the benefits of mild to moderate greatly outweigh the minor stress that it causes. Heavy weight lifting or extreme cardio will stress the body and can further work the Adrenal System.

Limit cardio and other exercise to 60 minutes at a time. After 60 minutes, your body starts to produce more cortisol to combat the stress placed upon the body. This can further negatively affect the Adrenal System.

15 – Minute Powernap or Break

If you are truly tired in the afternoon and need more stimulants to continue the rest of the day, try taking either a 15-minute powernap, or a general break during the afternoon. After working for a few hours, it's important to take a break to allow your brain the opportunity to relax and reorganize itself. Take deep breaths of air to saturate your blood with oxygen and provide release of stress. Depending on your job, you may be able to get away with more or less of a break. It's no question that many employers don't look highly among people napping in the middle of the office, but do the most you can to take a significant break.

Sitting in a quiet room, your car, or outside helps to remove you from job pressure so that you can relax and re-energize.

Limit / Eliminate Stimulants

Stimulants are not always the cause of Adrenal Fatigue, but they greatly speed up the process by synthetically causing the body to release stress hormones for energy. Since many people will not be able to completely give up caffeine immediately, it is important to limit the amount that you ingest each day. Caffeine is not entirely bad for us, coffee and tea, for example do have antioxidant properties, but more is never better. If you can avoid caffeine in its entirety, your health may be better off. However, if your morning cup of coffee is something that you enjoy, within limits, it is okay to have. Do your best to keep it to a small, and limit the sugar or artificial sweeteners that you add.

Sleep

Sleep is one of the most important functions of the human body. As goes with eating and drinking, the body also cannot survive without sleep. By maximizing the quality of the sleep that we get, our energy levels can provide us with the greatest amount of natural energy. Make sure your bedroom is conducive to sleep. It should be cool, completely dark, and in all honesty, there should not be a television, computer, or other modern-day distraction.

Diet

Since food is the fuel for your life, it is important to eat the foods that will fuel your body the best. Generally, the more processed and packaged a food is, the less beneficial it is to you. Green, leafy vegetables, nuts, fruits, fresh fish, chicken, lean beef, and whole grains are some of the examples of staples for a healthy diet. These foods contain fiber, antioxidants, vitamins, and minerals while most processed foods do not. All of them are readily available at your grocery store, and can typically be found for cheaper prices than processed foods.

You do not have to give up tasty foods, but work to limit your portions of the 'bad' and increase the 'good'.

Limit Sugar

It's becoming harder and harder to find foods that do not contain sugar, high fructose corn syrup, and artificial sweeteners. These foods have zero benefit to the body, but cause unnatural spikes in insulin levels, which ultimately lead to increased cortisol. These foods also cause us to crave them after a few hours.

The less sugar and sweeteners that you consume, the less that you will crave these foods and snacks. While artificial sweeteners are available, many people consider these to carry high health risks. It's ultimately your decision, but there is a wealth of information through creditable sources with little research.

Water

Water is necessary for providing solubility for many vitamins as well as for cellular activity and reproduction. While the common recommendation is 8 glasses of water (64 fl oz) per day, this will greatly vary by the climate where you live and your lifestyle. You should always be well hydrated to the point where your urine passes clear. Yellow urine is a sign of dehydration.

Soda is not a substitute for water. While it is primarily made up of water, it is not a suitable replacement for water.

Optimism and Stress

All of the above steps should help you to cope both with Adrenal Fatigue, as well as stress. While it is not possible to eliminate every stressor in your life, the better you handle stress in general, the less impact stress will take upon you. Stress often has a snowball effect: something small and less significant triggers all further stressors to be magnified. By the end of the day, your patience has run thin and you have no tolerance for even the most minor nuisance (such as yelling at traffic while driving home). Had you approached the earlier stressors in the day with a more optimistic approach, the rest of the day might be more carefree. If you don't let minor nuisances bother you, then technically, they are not even stressors anymore.

Nicotine

This goes without saying, but if you smoke, it's vital to quit. I will not run off endlessly explaining why you need to quit, it is common sense.

If you quit smoking right now, your body will be entirely free from nicotine in about 72-hours. All of the body's physical cravings and dependencies are gone after 72-hours. Past 72-hours, quitting smoking is entirely psychological and purely a mental addiction.

The Adrenal Fatigue Institute

After years of group research on Adrenal Fatigue, the Adrenal Fatigue Institute was finally born. The Adrenal Fatigue Institute's main objective is to continue to educate the public on the importance of a healthy Adrenal System and the true impact that the modern lifestyle is placing on our bodies.

What started out as a small idea has morphed into a full-fledge enterprise that provides people with an ability to gather as much information as possible on Adrenal Fatigue. We created **www.adrenalfatigueinstitute.com** as the back bone of the Adrenal Fatigue Institute. On the web site you are able to cross reference scientific studies with recent articles written on Adrenal fatigue. The Adrenal fatigue institute website gives you the ability to communicate with other people who suffer with adrenal fatigue through its online forums and communities. By continually updating the website with breaking news and studies on Adrenal Fatigue it allows you to always know if any new information is released that could help you. We also have a newsletter that goes out to all of our members with important nutrition and health updates.

The Adrenal Fatigue Institute has now grown to 20 full time employees working together to help provide as much information as possible to the general public about Adrenal Fatigue and how to cope with its debilitating effects. Our employees range from clinical researchers to telephone customer service reps that are available to take your questions Monday through Friday. We have made it our mission to help educate the public on this problem and to give you a forum where you can ask questions and find answers.

You Can Do It!

Your Adrenal System provides some of the most vital bodily-functions in your daily life. Man has survived for thousands of years partially in thanks to the Adrenal System and its ability to provide sudden energy to escape danger. Even though today's lifestyle is much 'safer' and man has the longest life expectancy ever, our bodies operate much the same as they did thousands of years ago. With our ever-changing lifestyles at a pace that never seems to stop, it is important that we allow our bodies the fundamental principles that they require to sustain healthy living.

It is important to understand that there are several causes of Adrenal Fatigue. While stimulants often appear to be the culprit, it is still entirely possible to suffer from Adrenal Fatigue without the use of any stimulants. At the end of the day, if our body is not rested and relaxed enough to counter the stressors and labor of the day, fatigue can certainly set in.

Many people think that fatigue is a just a minor issue that we can control with drugs and natural aids, but few people truly understand the implications of abusing our bodies through stress and a negative lifestyle. We hope that by reading this book, you will have a better understanding of fatigue, and how much pressure your lifestyle truly places upon your body. While Adrenal Fatigue will not affect everyone in their lifetime, it is a very simple situation to fall into if one places other obligations before his/her health.

References (sorted alphabetically):

(ISSN: 0022-5347)Department of Urology, University of Ulsan College of Medicine, Asan Medical Center, Seoul, Korea

A. Korneyev, B.S. Pan, A. Polo, E. Romeo, A. Guidotti, E. Costa Stimulation of brain pregnenolone synthesis by mitochondrial diazepam binding inhibitor receptor ligands in vivo, J. Neurochem. 61 (1993) 1515–1524.

A.C. Grobin, A.L. Morrow, 3a-Hydroxy-5a-pregnan-20-one levels and GABA receptor-mediated Cl flux across development in rat cerebral cortex, Dev. Brain Res. 131 (2001) 31–39.

A.E. Kelley, M. Winnock, L. Stinus, Amphetamine, apomorphine and investigatory behavior in the rat: analysis of the structure and of responses, Psychophysiology 88 (1986) 66–74.

A.Y. Deutch, R.J. Gruen, R.H. Roth, The effects of perinatal diazepam exposure on stress-induced activation of the mesotelence- phalic Akhondzadeh S. Tehran University of Medical Sciences, South Kargar Avenue, Tehran, Iran.

Altern Med Rev. 2000 Feb; 5(1), 64-71 Use of neurotransmitter precursors for treatment of depression., Meyers S.

Alexander G. Panossian. Alternative & Complementary Therapies. December 1, 2003, 9(6): 327-331. doi:10.1089/107628003322658610.

American College of Obstetricians and Gynecologists: Use of botanicals for management of menopausal symptoms. ACOG Practice Bulletin 28: 1-11, 2001.

Aqel MB. Relaxant effect of the volatile oil of Rosmarinus officinalis on tracheal smooth muscle. J Ethnopharmacol 1991;33:57–62.

Ashburn, L. L., Pub. Health Rep., U. S. P. H. S., 66,1337 (1940).

Azizov, A.P., and R.D. Seifulla, "[The effect of elton, leveton, fitoton and adapton on the work capacity of experimental animals]," Eksp Klin Farmakol (1998), 61(3):61-63

Barthelemy H, Chouvet B, Cambazard F. Skin and mucosal manifestations in vitamin deficiency.

Baumgaertel A. Alternative and controversial treatments for attention-deficit/hyperactivity disorder. Pediatr Clin of North Am . 1999;46(5):977-992

Bensky, Dan; et al. (2004). Chinese Herbal Medicine: Materia Medica, Third Edition. Eastland Press.

Bhattacharya A, Ghosal S, Bhattacharya SK. Anti-oxidant effect of Withania somnifera glycowithanolides in chronic footshock stress-induced perturbations of oxidative free radical scavenging enzymes and lipid peroxidation in rat frontal cortex and striatum. J Ethnopharmacol. 2001 Jan;74(1):1-6.

Bhattacharya, S., Goel R., Kaur, R., Ghosal, S. Anti-stress Activity of Sitoindosides VII and VIII, New Acylsterylglucosides from Withania Somnifera. Phytotherapy Res 1987;1:32-39.

Bob Garrison, Kerry Hughes. Alternative & Complementary Therapies. December 1, 2005, 11(6): 314-318. doi:10.1089/act.2005.11.314.

Bourin M, Bougerol T, Guitton B, Broutin E. A combination of plant extracts in the treatment of outpatients with adjustment disorder with anxious mood: controlled study versus placebo. Fundam Clin Pharmacol . 1997;11:127-132.

Britton, S. W., and Kline, R. F., Am. J. Physiol., 146,190 (1945).

Burdock GA. Review of the biological properties and toxicity of bee propolis. Food and Chemical Toxicology 36:347-363, 1998.

Carlson LA.Nicotinic acid: the broad-spectrum lipid drug. A 50th anniversary review. J Intern Med. 2005 Aug;258(2):94-114.

Castleman M. The Healing Herbs. New York: Bantam Books, 1991, 452–6.

Cauffield JS, Forbes HJ. Dietary supplements used in the treatment of depression, anxiety, and sleep disorders. Lippincotts Prim Care Pract . 1999; 3(3):290-304.

Cerny I, Pouzar V, Budesinsky M, Bicikova M, Hill M, Hampl R. Synthesis of [19- 2H3]-analogs of dehydroepiandrosterone and pregnenolone and their sulfates. Steroids. 2004 Mar;69(3):161-71.

Chen H, Tappel AL. Vitamin E, selenium, trolox C, ascorbic acid palmitate, acetylcysteine, coenzyme Q, beta-carotene, canthaxanthin, and (+)-catechin protect against oxidative damage to kidney, heart, lung and spleen. Free Radic Res. 1995 Feb;22(2):177-86.

Cytotoxic triterpenoids from the fruits of Zizyphus jujuba - jujube fruit. D Mowrey, Ph.D., The Scientific Validation of Herbal Medicine (New Canaan, CT: Keats Publishing), 1986. Pages102-103, 192-193.

D.M. Danks. Copper Deficiency in Humans. In: "Biological Roles of Copper." CIBA Foundation Symposium-79. Exerpta Medica, Amsterdam, 1980.

Daft, F. S., and Sebrell, W. H., Pub. Health Rep., U. S. P. H. S., 64,2247 (1939).
Daft, F. S., and Sebrell, W. H., Pub. Health Rep., U. S. P. H. S., 66,1333 (1940)

Davydov M, Krikorian AD. (October 2000). "Eleutherococcus senticosus (Rupr. & Maxim.) Maxim. (Araliaceae) as an adaptogen: a closer look.". Journal of Ethnopharmacology 72 (3): 345-393.

de Andrade E; de Mesquita AA; Claro Jde A; de Andrade PM; Ortiz V; Paranhos M; Srougi MStudy of the efficacy of Korean Red Ginseng in the treatment of erectile dysfunction. Sector of Sexual Medicine, Division of Urological Clinic of Sao Paulo University, Sao Paulo, Brazil.

Deane, H. W., and McKibbin, J. M., Endocrinology, 38, 385 (1946).
Deckert J, Nothen MM, Franke P. et al. Mol Psychiatry (1998) 3, 81-85.

DG Bailey, PhD, JMO Arnold, MD, HA Strong, PhD, C Munoz, MD, and JD Spence, MD. Effect of grapefruit Juice and naringin on nisoldipine pharmacokinetics. CLIN PHARMACOL THER 1993;54:589-94.

Dhuley JN. Nootropic-like effect of ashwagandha (Withania somnifera L.) in mice. Phytother Res. 2001 Sep;15(6):524-8.

Disorders of androgen synthesis--from cholesterol to dehydroepiandrosterone. Med Princ Pract. 2005;14 Suppl 1:58-68.

Review. dopamine system, Neuropsychopharmacology 2 (1989) 105– 114.

Eur J Pharmacol. 2002 Jun 12;445(3):221-9. Involvement of 5-hydroxytryptamine neuronal system in Delta(9)-tetrahydrocannabinol-induced impairment of spatial memory., Egashira N, Mishima K, Katsurabayashi S, Yoshitake T, Matsumoto Y, Ishida J, Yamaguchi M, Iwasaki K, Fujiwara M

FEBS Lett. 1999 Apr 16;449(1):45-8.

FEBS Lett. 1999 Apr 16;449(1):45-8.

Fenech M, Aitken C, Rinaldi J. Folate, vitamin B12, homocysteine status and DNA damage rate in young Australian adults. Carcinogenesis 1998;19:1163–71.

Fidanza A. Therapeutic action of pantothenic acid. Int J Vitam Nutr Res 1983;suppl 24:53–67 (review)

Fitday.com, Cyser Software, Inc, November 1, 2007.

Fuxe K, Ferré S, Zoli M. et al. Brain Res Rev (1998) 26, 258-273.

G Pouls, D.C., M Pouls, Ph.D., The Supplement Shopper (Tiburon, CA: Future Medicine Publishing, 1999). Pages 369-370.

G. Seematter, C. Binnert, L. Tappy. Metabolic Syndrome and Related Disorders. March 1, 2005, 3(1): 8-13. doi:10.1089/met.2005.3.8.

Grandhi, A. Comparative pharmacological investigation of ashwagandha and ginseng. Journal of Ethnopharmacology (Ireland), 1994: vol. 3, pp 131-135

Guardia T, Rotelli AE, Juarez AO, Pelzer LE. Anti-inflammatory properties of plant flavonoids. Effects of rutin, quercetin and hesperidin on adjuvant arthritis in rat. Farmaco 2001 Sep;56(9):683-7.

Gupta SK, Dua A, Vohra BP. Withania somnifera (Ashwagandha) attenuates antioxidant defense in aged spinal cord and inhibits copper induced lipid peroxidation and protein oxidative modifications. Drug Metabol Drug Interact. 2003;19(3):211-22.

Harkey MR, Henderson GL, Gershwin ME, Stern JS, Hackman RM. Variability in commercial ginseng products: an analysis of 25 preparations. Am J Clin Nutr. 2001;73:1101-1106.

HOAGLAND, HUDSON: Adventures in biological engineering. Science, 100:63, 1944.

Hong B; Ji YH; Hong JH; Nam KY; Ahn TYA double-blind crossover study evaluating the efficacy of korean red ginseng in patients with erectile dysfunction: a preliminary report. J Urol. 2002; 168(5):2070-3

Ip, S.P., et al., "Effect of a lignan-enriched extract of Schisandra chinensis on aflatoxin B1 and cadmium chloride-induced hepatotoxicity in rats," Pharmacol Toxicol (1996), 78(6):413-16

J Am Acad Dermatol. 1986 Dec;15(6):1263-74.

J Balch, M.D., P Balch, C.N.C., Prescription for Nutritional Healing (New York, NY: Avery) 2000. Pages 15-19.

J Balch, M.D., P Balch, C.N.C., Prescription for Nutritional Healing (New York, NY: Avery) 2000. Pages 646-647.

J Balch, M.D., P Balch, C.N.C., Prescription for Nutritional Healing (New York, NY: Avery) 2000. Page 89.

J Balch, M.D., P Balch, C.N.C., Prescription for Nutritional Healing (New York, NY: Avery) 2000. Pages 15-19.

J Clin Pharm Ther. 2001 Oct;26(5):363-7.

J Int Med Res. 1990 May-Jun;18(3):201-9. Double-blind study of 5-hydroxytryptophan versus placebo in the treatment of primary fibromyalgia syndrome., Caruso I, Sarzi Puttini P, Cazzola M, Azzolini V.

Jacobson KA, Gao ZG (2006). "Adenosine receptors as therapeutic targets". Nature reviews. Drug discovery 5 (3): 247–64.

K. Muneoka, T. Nakatsu, J. Fuji, T. Ogawa, M. Takigawa, Prenatal administration of nicotine results in dopaminergic alterations in the neocortex, Neurotoxicol. Teratol. 21 (1999) 603–609.

Kane, Emily. "From stressed to sane." Better Nutrition; May 2008, Vol. 70 Issue 5, p38-40

Kathy Abascal, Eric Yarnell. Alternative & Complementary Therapies. April 1, 2003, 9(2): 54-60. doi:10.1089/107628003321536959.

Katsumasa T. Muneoka, Yukihiko Shirayama, Yoshio Minabe, Morikuni Takigawa: Brain Research 956 (2002) 332–338

Keen CL and Zidenberg-Cherr S: Manganese. In Present Knowledge of Nutrition, 7th ed. Edited by EE Ziegler and LJ Filer.Washington, DC, ILSI Press, 1996; 334-343.

Kelly GS. Nutritional and botanical interventions to assist with the adaptation to stress. Alt Med Rev. 1999; 4(4):249-265.

Kelly GS. Nutritional and botanical interventions to assist with the adaptation to stress. Alt Med Rev. 1999; 4(4):249-265. Riboflavin and adrenal cortex. Nutr Rev. 1973 Mar;31(3):95-6.

Kelly GS. Nutritional and botanical interventions to assist with the adaptation to stress. Alt Med Rev. 1999;4(4):249-265.

Kuo SM. Antiproliferative potency of structurally distinct dietary flavonoids on human colon cancer cells. Cancer Lett 1996;110:41-8.

L.R. Baxter Jr., J.M. Schwartz, M.E. Phelps, J.C. Mazziotta, B.H. Guze, C.E. Selin, R.H. Gerner, R.M. Sumida, Reduction of prefrontal cortex glucose metabolism common to three types of depression, Arch. Gen. Psychiatry 46 (1989) 243-250.

Laber B, Maurer W, Scharf S, Stepusin K, Schmidt FS. Vitamin B6 biosynthesis: formation of pyridoxine 5'-phosphate from 4-(phosphohydroxy)-L-threonine and 1-deoxy-D-xylulose-5-phosphate by PdxA and PdxJ protein.

Laber B, Maurer W, Scharf S, Stepusin K, Schmidt FS. Vitamin B6 biosynthesis: formation of pyridoxine 5'-phosphate from 4-(phosphohydroxy)-L-threonine and 1-deoxy-D-xylulose-5-phosphate by PdxA and PdxJ protein.

Lakaye B, Makarchikov AF, Wins P, Margineanu I, Roland S, Lins L, Aichour R, Lebeau L, El Moualij B, Zorzi W, Coumans B, Grisar T, Bettendorff L.Human recombinant thiamine triphosphatase: purification, secondary

structure and catalytic properties. Int J Biochem Cell Biol. 2004
Jul;36(7):1348-64.

Lakaye B, Makarchikov AF, Wins P, Margineanu I, Roland S, Lins L, Aichour
R, Lebeau L, El Moualij B, Zorzi W, Coumans B, Grisar T, Bettendorff
L.Human recombinant thiamine triphosphatase: purification, secondary
structure and catalytic properties. Int J Biochem Cell Biol. 2004
Jul;36(7):1348-64.

Lee, I. S., Lee, H. K., Dat, N. T., Lee, M. S., Kim, J. W., Na, D. S., and Kim,
Y. H. Lignans with inhibitory activity against NFAT transcription from
Schisandra chinensis. Planta Med. 2003;69(1):63-64.

Leonardi R, Zhang YM, Rock CO, Jackowski S. Coenzyme A: back in action.
Prog Lipid Res. 2005 Mar-May;44(2-3):125-53. Epub 2005 Apr 20. Review.

Leonhardt W, et al: Impact of concentrations of glycated hemoglobin, alpha-
tocopherol, copper, and manganese on oxidation of low-density lipoproteins in
patients with type I diabetes, type II diabetes and control subjects. Clinica
Chimica Acta 1996; 254:173-186.

Levine J, Barak Y, Gonzalves M, et al. Double-blind, controlled trial of inositol
treatment of depression. Am J Psychiatry; 152:792-4, 1995.

Li, P.C., et al., "Schisandra chinensis-dependent myocardial protective action
of sheng-mai-san in rats," Am J Chin Med (1996), 24(3-4):255-62

Life Extension Media, Disease Prevention and Treatment, Third Edition
(Hollywood, FL: Life Extension Foundation) 2000. Page 21.

Liske E, Hanggi MD, Henneicke-von Zepelin HH, et al.: Physiological
investigation of a unique extract of black cohosh (Cimicifugae racemosae
rhizoma): a 6-month clinical study demonstrates no systemic estrogenic effect.
Journal of Women's Health & Gender-Based Medicine 11: 163-174, 2002.

Liu, G. T. Pharmacological actions and clinical use of fructus schizandrae. Chin Med.J.(Engl.) 1989;102(10):740-749.

Lowry, 0. H., Lopez, J. A., and Bessey, 0. A., J. Biol. Chem., 180, 609 (1945).

M Ebadi, J Marwah, R Chopra, Mitochondrial Ubiquinone (CoenzymeQ10): Biochemical, Functional, Medical and Therapeutic Aspects in Human Health and Diseases, Volume 1 (Scottsdale, AZ: Prominent Press) 2001. Page186.

M Murray, N.D., Encyclopedia of Nutritional Supplements (Rocklin, CA: Prima Publishing), 1996. Pages 81-136.

M Murray, N.D., J. Pizzorno, N.D., Encyclopedia of Natural Medicine (Rocklin, CA: Prima Publishing), 1991. Pages 97-98.

M Pouls, Ph.D., Townsend Letter for Doctors and Patients, "Oral Chelation and Nutritional Replacement Therapy for Chemical and Heavy Metal Toxicity and Cardiovascular Disease" July 1999. Pages 82-91.

M Werbach, M.D., M Murray, N.D., Botanical Influences on Illness (Tarzana, CA: Third Line Press), 1994. Pages 10-11

Maile Pouls, Ph.D., from clinical experience 1986-2001.

Maughan Rj, Evans SP. Effects of pollen extract upon adolescent swimmers. Br J Sports Med. 1982 Sep;16(3):142-5

Meltzer HY. Neuropsychopharmacology (1999) 21, 106S-115S.

Moro S, Gao ZG, Jacobson KA, Spalluto G. Progress in the pursuit of therapeutic adenosine receptor antagonists. Med Rev Res. 2006 Mar;26(2):131-59.

Muller CE, Scior T:Adenosine receptors and their modulators. Parm Acta Helv. 1993 Sep;68(2):77-111

Neilsen FH: Ultratrace elements. In Modern Nutrition in Health and Disease, 8th ed. Edited by ME Shils, JA Olson, M Shike. Philadelphia, Lea and Febiger, 1994; 269-286.

Nelson, A. A., Pub. Health Rep., U. S. P. II. S., 64,2250 (1939).

Nolan, K., "Copper Toxicity Syndrome", J. Orthomolecular Psychiatry, 12:4, p.270-282.

Nordic Journal of Psychiatry, 2007 V. 61, No. 5, "SHR-5 Rhodiola rosea and the Treatment of Depression" by V.Darbinyan, G.Aslanyan, E.Amroyan, E.Gabrielyan , C.Malmstro, A.Panossian, The PBM Clinic, Institute of Health Competence, Stockholm-Globen, Sweden

Maslova L.V. et al. (1994) "The cardioprotective and antiadrenergic activity of an extract of Rhodiola rosea in stress" Eksp Klin Farmakol 57(6): 61-6

Nowak M, Swietochowska E, Wielkoszynski T, Marek B, Kos-Kudla B, Szapska B, Kajdaniuk D, Glogowska-Szelag J, Sieminska L, Ostrowska Z, Koziol H, Klimek J. Homocysteine, vitamin B12, and folic acid in age-related macular degeneration. Eur J Ophthalmol. 2005 Nov-Dec;15(6):764-7.

P.A. Borea, K. Varani, A. Dalpiaz, A. Capuzzo, E. Fabbri, A.P. Ijzerman, Full and partial agonistic behaviour and thermodynamic binding parameters of adenosine A1 receptor ligands, Eur. J. Pharmacol. 267 (1994) 55–61.

P.J. Marangos, J. Patel, A.M. Martino, M. Dilli, J.P. Boulenger, Differential binding properties of adenosine receptor agonists and antagonists in brain, J. Neurochem. 41 (1983) 367–374.

Panda S, Kar A. Evidence for free radical scavenging activity of Ashwagandha root powder in mice. Indian J Physiol Pharmacol. 1997 Oct;41(4):424-6

Panossian AG, Oganessian AS, Ambartsumian M, Gabrielian ES, Wagner H, Wikman G. Effects of heavy physical exercise and adaptogens on nitric oxide content in human saliva. Phytomedicine. 1999 Mar;6(1):17-26.

Parsons B, Togasaki DM, Kassir S. et al. J Neurochem (1995) 65, 2057-2064.

Patak P, Willenberg HS, Bornstein SR. Vitamin C is an important cofactor for both adrenal cortex and adrenal medulla. Endocr Res. 2004 Nov;30(4):871-5.

Petkov, V.D. et. al. (1986) "Effects of alcohol aqueous extract from Rhodiola rosea L. roots on learning and memory" Acta Physiol Pharmacol Bulg 12(1): 3-16

PINCUS, GREGORY, and HOAGLAND, HUDSON: Effects of administered pregnenolone on fatiguing psychomotor performance. J. of. Aviat. Med., 15:98, 135, 1944.

PINCUS, GREGORY, and HOAGLAND, HUDSON: Steroid excretion and the stress of flying. J. of Aviat. Med., 14: 173, 1943.

Pinna A, Wardas J, Cristalli G. et al. Brain Res (1997) 759, 41-49.
Planta Med. 2003 Nov; 69(11):1051-4.

Prasad AS. Zinc in human health: an update. J Trace Elem Exp Med 1998;11:63–87

R. Guillet, C. Kellogg, Neonatal exposure to therapeutic caffeine alters the ontogeny of adenosine A1 receptors in brain of rats, Neuropharmacology 30 (1991) 489–496.

R.F. Bruns, J.H. Fergus, E.W. Badger, J.A. Bristol, L.A. Santay, J.D. Hartman, S.J. Hays, C.C. Huang, Binding of the A –selective adenosine antagonist 8-cyclopentyl-1,3-dipropylxanthine to rat brain membranes, Naunyn-Schmiedebergs Arch. Pharmacol. 335 (1987) 59–63.

RA Passwater, Ph.D., The Nutrition Superbook: Volume I: The Antioxidants, The Nutrients That Guard the Body Against Cancer, Heart Disease, Arthritis and Allergies- and Even Slow the Aging Process (New Canaan, CT: Keats Publishing) 1995. Pages 4-8, 184-186, 363.

Rahman MK, Nagatsu T, Sakurai T, Hori S, Abe M, Matsuda M (1982). "Effect of pyridoxal phosphate deficiency on aromatic L-amino acid decarboxylase activity with L-DOPA and L-5-hydroxytryptophan as substrates in rats". Jpn. J. Pharmacol. 32 (5): 803-11.

Ralli, E. P., and Graef, I., Endocrinology, 32, 1 (1943).
Ray JG, Cole DE. Vitamin B12 and homocysteine. CMAJ. 2005 Nov 22;173(11):1359-60.

Riboflavin and adrenal cortical metabolism. Nutr Rev. 1960 Jul;18:221-2.

Roberts, Carol L. "Adrenal Fatigue: An American Epidemic," New Times Naturally!, Dec2007

Russel RM. A minimum of 13,500 deaths annually from coronary artery disease could be prevented by increasing folate intake to reduce homocysteine levels. JAMA 1996;275:1828–9.

Ryan, Suzie et. al,. "The First 72 Hours". Freedom. November 1, 2007. <http://groups.msn.com/FreedomFromTobaccoQuitSmokingNow/the1st72hour s.msnw>

S Felice, M.D., The Carnitine Defense (Rodale) 1999. Page 89.
S. Fisher, R. Guillet, Neonatal caffeine alters passive avoidance retention in rats in an age- and gender-related manner, Dev. Brain Res. 98 (1997) 145–149.

Shirayama, Yukihiko2, CA; Muneoka, Katsumasa T.1; Takigawa, Morikuni1; Minabe, Yoshio: Adenosine A2A, 5-HT1A and 5-HT7 receptor in neonatally pregnenolone-treated rats [Neuropharmacology And Neurotoxicology] Neuroreport:Volume 12(17)4 December 2001pp 3773-3776

Somer E. The Essential Guide to Vitamins and Minerals. New York: Harper, 1995, 70–2.

Sosnova TL, Golubev VV, Plekhanova NA, Afanas'ev AN. [Stimulating effects of eleuterococcus and Chinese schizandra used for prevention of visual fatigue during work connected with color discrimination] Gig Sanit. 1984 Dec;(12):7-9.

Soulimani R, Younos C, Jarmouni S, Bousta D, Misslin R, Mortier F. Behavioural effects of Passiflora incarnata L. and its indole alkaloid and flavonoid derivatives and maltol in the mouse. J Ethnopharmacol. 1997;57(1):11-20.

Stockton, CA: Therapeutic Research Faculty Publishing) 1999. Page 832.

Sun, H.D., et al., "Nigranoic acid, a triterpenoid from Schisandra sphaerandra that inhibits HIV-1 reverse transcriptase," J Nat Prod (1996), 59(5):525-27

Therapeutic Research Faculty, Natural Medicines Comprehensive Database Stockton, CA: Therapeutic Research Faculty Publishing) 1999. Page 832

Therapeutic Research Faculty, Natural Medicines Comprehensive Database Turgeon SM, Pollack AE, Schusheim L. et al. Brain Res (1996) 707, 75-80

Tori Hudson. Alternative & Complementary Therapies. June 1, 2006, 12(3): 132-135. doi:10.1089/act.2006.12.132.

Upton, R, ed. Black Cohosh Rhizome Actaea racemosa L. syn. Cimicifuga racemosa (L.) Nutt. Standards of analysis, quality control, and therapeutics. American Herbal

Vinson JA, Bose P. Comparative bioavailability to humans of ascorbic acid alone or in a citrus extract. Am J Clin Nutr 1988;48:601–4.

Wang RY, Liang X. Neuropsychopharmacology (1998) 19, 74-85.

Wang YH, Gao JP, Chen DF. [Determination of lignans of Schisandra medicinal plants by HPLC] Zhongguo Zhong Yao Za Zhi. 2003 Dec;28(12):1155-60.

Wiesel LL, Barritt AS, Stumpe WM. The synergistic action of para-aminobenzoic acid and cortisone in the treatment of rheumatoid arthritis. Am J Med Sci 1951;222:243–8.

Winston, David; Steven Maimes (2007). Adaptogens: Herbs for Strength, Stamina, and Stress Relief. Healing Arts Press.

Wurtman RJ, Hefti F, Melamed E. Precursor control of neurotransmitter synthesis. Pharmacol Rev. 1981; 32:315-335.

Y. Shirayama, K. Hashimoto, T. Higuchi, Y. Minabe, Subchronic treatment with methamphetamine and phencyclidine differentially alters the adenosine A1 and A2A receptors in the prefrontal cortex, hippocampus, and striatum of the rat, Neurochem. Res. 26 (2001) 363–368.

Yang LQ, Wu XY, Xu ZQ, Hou HR, Fu HZ.[Research progress on determination of lignans from Schiandra chinensis and its preparations] Zhongguo Zhong Yao Za Zhi. 2005 May;30(9):650-3.

Zakir Ramazanov, Z. et al. (1999) "New secrets of effective natural stress and weight management, using Rhodiola rosea and Rhodendron caucasicum" ATN/Safe Goods Publishing, CT

Zal HM. Five herbs for depression, anxiety, and sleep disorders. Uses, benefits, and adverse effects. Consultant . 1999;3343-3349.

Zempleni J, Mock DM. Biotin biochemistry and human requirements. J Nutr Biochem 1999;10:128–38.

Z.P. Liu, B. Yu, J.S. Huo, C.Q. Lu, J.S. Chen. Journal of Medicinal Food. September 1, 2001, 4(3): 171-178. doi:10.1089/109662001753165756.